Indexers and Index
in Fact and Fiction

Indexers and Indexes

in Fact and Fiction

Edited by

Hazel K. Bell

with a Foreword by

A.S. Byatt

The British Library

Published in 2001 by
The British Library
96 Euston Road
London NW1 2DB

© in this anthology, 2001 Hazel K. Bell
© in the text, 2001 Hazel K. Bell and other named copyright owners
© in the Foreword, 2001 A.S. Byatt
© in the front cover illustration, 2001 Dean Munson

British Library Cataloguing in Publication Data
A catalogue record for this book is available from The British Library

ISBN 0 7123 4729 1

Designed and typeset by Peter and Alison Guy
Printed in Great Britain by Biddles

Contents

35 Let me help:
W. E. Tate, *The English Village Community and the Enclosure Movements*
(1967)

36 Sequential subheadings:
Desmond Ryan, *The Fenian Chief: A Biography of James Stephens*
(1967)

37 The hit direct:
Bernard Levin, *The Pendulum Years* (1970)

38 Indigestible index:
Magnus Pyke, *Man and Food* (1970)

39 The Frank Muir index:
The Frank Muir Book: An Irreverent Companion to Social History
(1976)

40 Prejudicial introduction:
Peter Schickele, *The Definitive Biography of P.D.Q. Bach* (1976)

41 Forbearance:
Hugh Vickers, *Great Operatic Disasters* (1979)

42 Literally food for thought?
Equality by Keith Joseph and Jonathan Sumption (1979)

43 Egoism rampant:
Joseph Bonnano, *A Man of Honour* (1983)

44 Kiss and have it told:
Pepys's Diary (1983 edition)

45 It didn't work out that way ...
Cerf and Navasky, *The Experts Speak* (1984)

46 Monstrous entry:
Guide to Britain's Nature Reserves (1984)

47 Conductor's contempt:
Hunter Davies, *The Good Guide to the Lakes* (1986)

48 The terminology of the shrew:
Dale Spender, *Scribbling Sisters* (1986)

49 Cramming it onto a page:
Patrick Barlow, *All the World's a Globe, or from Lemur to Cosmonaut:
Desmond Olivier Dingle's Concise History of the Human Race* (1987)

50 Guess who?
A. Summers and S. Dorril, *Honeytrap: The Secret Worlds of Stephen Ward*
(1987)

51 Political affiliation no secret:
Paul Slansky, *The Clothes Have No Emperor: The Reagan Years*
(1989)

52 Nudge, nudge:
Julian Barnes, *Letters from London 1990-1995* (1995)

53 No fury like it:
Margaret Cook, *A Slight and Delicate Creature* (1999)

54 Inveighing against the computer:
Clifford Stoll, *High Tech Heretic* (1999)

An index is customarily regarded as an arrangement of signposts pointing the way to alphabetically analysed textual content, but may effectively serve more imaginative purposes: to relieve the text of overburdening detail, to replace footnotes, to sharpen the perspective of the text, to supplement as well as elucidate textual content. Above all, it may be made so readable that one may begin *with the index, deriving from it such pleasure as will stimulate eagerness to turn back to the text, perhaps piecemeal rather than as a continuous whole ... I prefer the Index which has a life of its own, which may pride itself on being the child of imagination, and which should enable us to spend a peaceful evening in bed, reading such an Index, as if we were reading a good novel.*

William S. Heckscher,
The unconventional index and its merits,
The Indexer 13 (1) April 1982, 7–25

Foreword by A. S. Byatt

It takes time and experience to become one of those who, choosing books in a bookshop, or from the shelves of a library, learn to turn first to the index. From a good index it is possible to find out rapidly what is covered in a book, which subjects are covered in the greatest depth, and to get a 'feel' for the shape and style. Experience of unreliable, or tendentious, or badly planned indexes causes us to see slowly just what skill and intelligence goes into a good one. Later still, one comes to admire the index as a work of art.

An index is many things. It is a map, a mnemonic, a digest. When I write lectures, or book reviews, I tend to make my own arbitrary chronological digest of the books inside the endpapers, pinpointing the page where Anna Karenina sees the man tapping the train wheels, or Coleridge defines a symbol. Such digests are mnemonics also, and the secret of preparing for exams was, in my case, to reduce such lists to smaller lists of mnemonics, and make meta-mnemonics for groups of specific mnemonics, until I could call up information in order, like fish on hooks on the end of lines. It took me a long time to realise that much of this work has already been done by a good indexer. (And perhaps in any case the brain needs to do its own sorting, arranging and reducing.) The order of an index is conferred of course, arbitrarily and often comically or beautifully, by the order of the alphabet. There has been a pedagogic fashion for not teaching the alphabet to children, out of a current fear of 'rote learning'. But the human mind works by internalising such arbitrary and useful tools, as a kind of grid onto which knowledge can be arranged and from which it can be retrieved. I am daily grateful that at my elementary school we learned to chant the alphabet both forwards and backwards.

Indexes can be made of many subjects, fact and fictions, whole literatures and minutiae. A concordance to the Bible is an indispensable short-cut for sermon writers, theologians and those curious about which subjects came up most frequently in the minds of scribes and concordance-makers. Looking up 'women' in Cruden's Concordance opens a world of ripped up children, warnings against lewdness, several injunctions by St Paul against allowing women to speak in churches, or govern anything, and themes of wailing, original sin, and obedience. There are also the Magnificat, and the Song of Songs. A concordance to the works of a poet can show quickly which themes recur in his or her work. The index to a dictionary of quotations is in itself a poem, a kind of meta-index, in which can be found gatherings of adumbrated poems about moons, or suns, fire, wolves, tea-kettles, politicians or whatever else the minds of men return to through the centuries.

It might be thought that modern technology, the CD and the search engine, had made indexers less necessary, or even redundant. I remember a professor of Ancient Greek telling me that all works of ancient Greek literature were now on a single CD. He said that theses that had taken students years to research – on the scattered references to certain illnesses for instance – could now be done almost at a touch. Such machines are wonderful, but are not a substitute for the contact with another human intelligence made when one consults a good index. Their assistance produces anomalies – my friend Jenny Uglow, the biographer, speaks with pleasure of good chronological guides to lives, within indexes, and the sheer unuseful irritation produced by rendering these sub-entries in alphabetical form – beginning with 'Aunt Amy's visit in 1868,' not because it came early, but because it begins with 'A'.

I first met Hazel Bell when she wrote to me with a proposal for indexing one of my novels. She was professionally interested in the difference between an index to fiction and an index to a true history or to a biography. She was interested in the differences between the kinds of entries needed for different members of an imaginary family, and one in a real biography. She has made indexes of three of a quartet of novels of which I am at the moment finishing the fourth. She writes interestingly about how she revises, making entries for themes and symbols that begin to recur, selecting incidents that appear to need special references. I was a little anxious – although intrigued – when she began. In fact I have found her indexes invaluable for keeping track of chronology, and not only of chronology but of thematic shapings, in the writing of the fourth book, and have come to appreciate just how useful and accurate a map of the workings of my own mind she has made. Like many writers I dislike rereading my own work – which in the case of a serial novel is nevertheless inevitable – and it is illuminating and incredibly useful to have a quick guide.

I make the notes for these novels in a series of notebooks, which were started on before the computer age. I tried to index the notebooks in a meta-notebook with an alphabetical guide like an address book but it couldn't be done. It is, however, easy to do on the computer, with the beautiful sliding expansive flexibility of the word-wrapped document. It begins **Acidale, Agatha, Alexander, Alkon, Altizer, Altruism, Animals, Anti-University, Archer, Artaud, Asylum, Auden, Augustine**... and ends **Turing, Twins, Waddington, Whistling, Wijnnobel, Oscar Wilde, Bernard Williams, George C. Williams, Harry Williams, Wilkie, Wittgenstein, Wolpert, Wordsworth, Wren-Lewis, J.Z. Young, Smir Zeki, Zodiac.** The omissions are as interesting as the inclusions. Several of the entries have an agonised note that they are Late Entries, meaning that I hadn't realised that the subject was going to need its own entry. All this increases my admiration for Hazel Bell's accomplishment. She mentions also what is probably the most useful index to fiction, the superb critical apparatus of the Pléiade edition of Proust's *A La Recherche du Temps Perdu*, without which attempting to write closely about Proust's text would be daunting. This index is a delight, and starts me reading obscure passages I had quite forgotten every time I look up something I had half-remembered. Indexes are a kind of *Sortes Virgilianae*, a place where the pleasure of sorting and ordering meets the opposite pleasure of the random, the inconsequential and the chancy. The word 'sort' is in itself interesting – 'le sort' in French is destiny or fate, but this derives from a lottery.

Everyone must have their own favourite indexes. Mine is the ornate and poetic index to Burton's *Anatomy of Melancholy*, included here, which I always associate in my mind with the richness and eloquent overloading of the indexes to the many versions of *The Golden Bough*, which are in themselves a magical cosmogonic compression. J.L. Lowes, in *The Road to Xanadu*, pointed out how the 'hooks and eyes' of Coleridge's imagination operated by a system of constant cross-referencing, always following up footnotes. The index to Coleridge's *Biographia Literaria*, edited by J. Shawcross in 1907, is a pleasure to use, though it does not have entries under 'symbol' and 'metaphor', an omission which I constantly forget and am repeatedly irritated by. But the workings of Coleridge's mind can be felt in the entries. For instance:

Philosophy, definition of, i.94; nomenclature of, 108, 188; golden rule for study of, 160; criterion of fitness for, 162; not intelligible to the ordinary mind, 164-9, 173; the pure, 164; moral side of, 172; the organ of, 173; freedom a ground of, 185; popular, its predominance and dangers, 192; specific genius required for, 198; and poetry, ii, 270; mechanical, the, see Mechanical.

This is infinitely more use than a mere list of page numbers, and conveys a whole tone of mind.

I also love the leisurely, thorough indexes of the great Victorians and very early moderns. Karl Pearson's enormous three-volume *Life of Sir Francis Galton* has a wonderful index full of extra information and useful lists – for instance, under I, the splendid list of Instruments designed by F.G.:

Instruments designed by F.G. Anthropometric, psychometric, meteorological et al. Many unidentified devices, and drawings of devices, whose purpose may now only be divined are collectively known in the Anthropometric laboratory as Galton's Toys.

Drill pantograph. Weather balloon. A lock. A lamp. A balance. A printing telegraph. A device for compounding six objects. A hyperscope. A wave engine. A heliostat. A 'Tactor' machine. A machine for optical combination of images. An Iceland spar compounder. A measurement of resemblance machine. An instantaneous attitude snapper. Spectacles for divers. Whistles for high notes. A Pocket registrator. An instrument for testing the perception of tint differences. An instrument for measuring the movement of a limb.

Galton's own indexing is thorough. I am amused by the one in his 1872 *Art of Travel (Or, Shifts and Contrivances Available in Wild Countries)*. This was a frequently updated and reprinted bestseller, and its index needed to be quickly useful in emergencies. It produces a splendid blend of the practical with the exoticism of juxtaposition which is one of the greatest pleasures of reading indexes – of which Hazel Bell has collected many brilliant examples.

Trees (see TIMBER), as shelter, 132; to mark, 289; to fell with fire, 90, 145; to hollow with fire, 93; as signs of neighbouring water, 212; to climb, 43; to steer by, 287; to make caches in, 301; boughs bent as accumulators, 324; bark to strip, 146; tree-bridges, 110

There follow a series of words with one or two page references:

Trektows (traces), Triangulation, table for, by chords, Trenches, for cooking, Trimmers, Trous de loup, Trowsers, Tschudi, Dr, Tulcban bishops, Turf sceen against wind, Turnscrew in pocket-knife, Turpentine, Turtle, water in its pericardium, Tylor, Mr, Tyndall, Professor, Uganda, thornwreath, Ulysses, Underground huts...

There are many other ingenious examples of indexes well-done and ill-done in this collection. Before I read it I had not considered the use of an index as a biased political bludgeon against the book it is attached to. I had never seen a complete example of the index which simply cross-refers to itself, like a house of mirrors. I was delighted by Douglas Matthews's index to Frank Muir, which recreates – in a new art form – the comedy of the book. Mr Matthews was the Librarian of the London Library, and writes indexes with pleasure in both order and oddity. The unique and idiosyncratic shelving system of that Library has the double quality of the best indexes. It represents order – it is helpful, it leads you to what you were trying to find, and also to what you needed, but did not know you needed to find. It also has the delightfully mad quality of heterogeneous things linked violently together by the arbitrary order of the alphabet. Dancing, Deaf and Dumb, Death, Dentistry, Devil and Demonology, Distribution, Dogs, Domestic Servants, Dreams. In this it resembles the lovely lists of Jorge Luis Borges, inventor of the Library of Babel, and recorder of the list of strange beasts in 'a certain Chinese encyclopaedia' which he describes in 'The Analytical Language of John Wilkins'. Animals are divided into

Those that belong to the Emperor
Embalmed ones
Those that are trained
Suckling pigs
Mermaids
Fabulous ones
Stray dogs
Those included in the present classification
Those that tremble as if they were mad
Innumerable ones
Those drawn with a very fine camel-hair brush
Others
Those that have just broken a flower vase
Those that from a long way off look like flies.

This list is a *locus classicus* of classification. When I thought of including it, I could not remember which of Borges's writings was the source. The Society of Indexers, through its web site, came to my rescue – an entirely appropriate eventuality. The first emails referred me to Foucault, who said it 'shattered all the familiar land-marks of his thought'. Subsequent correspondents identified its source exactly and pointed out that it had been cited by anthropologists, ethnographers, German teachers, postmodern feminists, Australian museum curators and artists. I tried to check it in a French edition of Foucault's *Les Mots et les Choses* and found to my amazement that this stringently complex work has no index. I remembered my own irritation with other French works lacking this essential resource. This in turn led to the discovery of Bella Hass Weinberg's article in *The Indexer* (Vol 22 no 1 April 2000) on Book Indexes in France, in which she explains that although the French invented the index, modern French publishers do not see the need for them. They should reconsider. A good index is a work of art and science, order and chance, delight and usefulness. This anthology is full of all these.

Introductory note

The history of indexes

The origins of indexing, as an aid to finding specific passages in books, are indistinct; before the invention of printing in the mid-15th century, manuscripts and scrolls were not paginated and no two of them were exactly the same.[1] Nevertheless, lists of terms referring to items in manuscript texts, rearranged in alphabetical order, did appear, compiled primarily for the advancement of religion.[2] An early example is that to the *Apothegmata*, a list of the sayings of various Greek Fathers, in the 5th century. Biblical concordances appeared in the 7th and 8th centuries; alphabetical lists of words and phrases from the Hebrew Bible were compiled by the 10th-century Masoretes;[3] and a 'primitive subject index' was supplied to the canonical collection of Christian laws of Cardinal Deusdedit, in the late 11th century. In the 13th century, the first Christian citation index, 'a concordance to the incidental passages in the writings of the fathers', appeared, while *real-concordances*, as mediaevalists call them, with theological concepts classified in a hierarchical sequence, were produced in France: the first was *Concordancia morales bibliorum*. By the mid-13th century, too, alphabetical subject indexes to Aristotle's Ethics and natural works had been compiled, as well as indexes to the Old and New Logic.[4] Alternating blue and red headwords was a common feature of mediaeval Latin indexes, which enhanced the clarity of these tools.[5]

The oldest *printed* indexes are found in two editions of St Augustine's *De arte praedicandi*, published by Fust & Schoeffer (the print-

1. Wellisch, Hans H. Incunabula indexes. *The Indexer* 19 (1) April 1994, 3-12
2. Weinberg, Bella Hass. Indexes and religion: reflections on research in the history of indexes. *The Indexer* 21 (3) April 1999, 111-18
3. Weinberg, Bella Hass. Who invented the index? IFLA Conference proceedings, August 2000. IFLA web site.
4. Rouse, Richard H. and Mary A. Rouse (1979) *Preachers, florilegia and sermons.* Pontifical Institute of Mediaeval Studies, 13; cited in Book indexes in France: medieval specimens and modern practices. Bella Hass Weinberg. *The Indexer* 22 (1) April 2000, 2-13
5. Weinberg, Bella Hass. Who invented the index? IFLA Conference proceedings, August 2000. IFLA web site.

ers of Gutenberg's Bible) in Mainz, and by Mentelin in Strassburg, probably in the early 1460s.[6] Printing enabled the production of identical copies of books, with page numbers, making possible indexes in their now traditional form, and soon these began to be compiled; 83 are to be found in books printed before 1500.[7] The first known *dated* index appeared in 1468 in *Speculum vitae*, a moral treatise printed by Sweynheym and Pannartz in Rome. The earliest examples of indexes in more than one language and in several scripts are those found in herbals of the late 15th and early 16th century, when name and subject indexes alphabetically arranged gradually developed. The herbals, medico-botanical works, contained extensive name and subject indexes, often in more than one language and sometimes even in more than one script, with plant names first in Latin, then in Greek'.[8] The second edition of Barbaro's Latin translation of Dioscorides' *Materia medica*, published in 1529, constituted a major advance in the art of indexing. It included both an extensive index of plant names printed on eight pages in two columns, arranged in strict alphabetical order throughout each name, and a subject index of six pages in three columns to a page, preserving Greek script as well as Latin.[9]

By the turn of the 16th century the making of indexes had advanced from rather crude and poorly arranged listings to carefully alphabetized, analytical and comprehensive keys to textual information, including elaborate typographical arrangement of items in different scripts.[10] However, the art of indexing was not very highly developed in general before 1550: the alphabetical arrangement of entries rarely extended beyond the second letter of the first word.[11] Nor, at that period, was indexing always regarded as necessarily a good thing, nor information as something proper to be sought out. Far from it: in 1544 the first man to prepare a concordance to the Bible was sentenced to be burned at the stake for heresy, possibly 'for fear that Divine Revelation would be reduced

6. Wellisch, Hans H. The oldest printed indexes. *The Indexer* 15 (2) Oct. 1986, 73-82
7. Wellisch, Hans H. Incunabula indexes. *The Indexer* 19 (1) April 1994, 3-12
8. Wellisch, Hans H. Early multilingual and multiscript indexes in herbals. *The Indexer* 11 (2) Oct. 1978, 81-102
9. Wellisch, Hans H. The oldest printed indexes. *The Indexer* 15 (2) Oct. 1986, 73-82
10. Ibid.
11. Ibid.

to human proportions and the canonical shape of the Bible be challenged'.[12] Published in 1564, the *Index librorum prohibitorum* 'was intended, not to promote or reveal, but to conceal information from good Catholics who were not supposed to read the books listed in' it.[13]

The oldest index continuously in print is probably the *Complete concordance to the Holy Scriptures* compiled by Alexander Cruden, first published in 1737.[14]

Periodicals began to appear in Britain in the 17th century, and to be indexed.[15] By the mid-18th century, subject indexes accumulating multiple scattered references were appearing in journals; the *Monthly Chronicle* (1728-31) was the first British periodical to produce multiple indexes. Such bringing together of material in one place was a welcome new development in information retrieval. By the end of the 18th century, indexes were recognized as instruments in their own right for the systematization of knowledge.

The indexers

Indexes to books at first were usually compiled by their authors, until the advent of the professional indexer in the 18th century. Samuel Ayscough, who compiled the indexes to his *Catalogue of the Manuscripts preserved in the British Museum, hitherto undescribed, and consisting of five thousand volumes* (published in 1782 in two quarto volumes) as well as to long runs of periodicals, was the first person to be described in the *Dictionary of National Biography* as an 'indexmaker'.[16]

In 1877, in London, The Index Society was formed, 'with the immediate object of compiling Subject Indexes and Indexes of standard books of facts ... with the ultimate object of building up a general Index of Universal Literature'.[17] Its members included Sir

12. Weinberg, Bella Hass. Indexes and religion: reflections on research in the history of indexes. *The Indexer* 21 (3) April 1999, 111-18
13. Wellisch, Hans H. 'Index' – the word, its history, meanings and usages. *The Indexer* 13 (3) April 1983, 147-51
14. Farrow, John. Alexander Cruden and his Concordance. *The Indexer* 20 (1) April 1996, 55-6
15. Johnson, Peter. Printed indexes to early British periodicals. *The Indexer* 16 (3), April 1989, 147-55
16. Anderson, M. D. Samuel Ayscough, 1745-1804. *The Indexer* 15 (3) April 1987, 157-8
17. Piggott, Mary. How the Index Society began – and ended. *The Indexer* 22 (1) April 2000, 33-5

George Grove, John L. Roget (son of the originator of *Roget's Thesaurus*), and Walter Skeat, the philologist, with Dr Henry Benjamin Wheatley, clerk and librarian to the Royal Society, as Honorary Secretary. Wheatley wrote the Society's first publication, *What Is An Index?*, in 1878, and drew up their 'Rules for obtaining uniformity in the indexes of books'. But by 1890 the Society was in financial dificulties, and merged with the British Record Society.

The membership of the Index Society had consisted of gentlemen all, but by the dawn of the 20th century indexing was seen as suitable work to be undertaken by women. In 1892 the *Englishwoman's Review* (15 October) gave notice that Miss Nancie Baily had opened an office in London's Bedford Square 'which will undertake all kinds of indexing ... The need for a good index is universally recognized, but the difficulty of getting one made in time by a person who has studied indexing as an art is often insuperable,' proclaimed her advertisement. Miss Baily had been indexer of *Hansard's Parliamentary Debates* from 1889-91, and her new office had 'already met with much success'. In 1895 Mary Petherbridge, a librarian, indexer of the records of the East India Company, the Drapers' Company, and *The Ladies' Field*, set up The Secretarial Bureau in London, first in the Strand, later in Conduit Street, 'for supplying help and advice in connection with letters and documents'; the Bureau provided indexers as well as secretaries and translators.[18] In 1904 she published a booklet, *The Technique of Indexing*, which included advice on indexing as a career: 'Indexing is not an easy profession, but it is an interesting one. ... The outlook is promising, but only for the trained worker. ... Indexing posts – some of them very well paid – are increasing yearly. Government has lately added an official indexer to the staff of certain of the Government offices.' According to the Women's Institute's *Dictionary of Employments Open to Women*, published in 1898, an indexer could then earn £125 plus a year.

Nineteen years later Petherbridge wrote an article entitled 'Indexing As A Profession for *Women*' [*sic*] that appeared in *Good Housekeeping* in September 1923. She explained:

> The indexer works quietly in the background; ... analysing each sentence, each paragraph, and writing up the index slips of all the facts and names there mentioned. ... picking out the essential fact hidden beneath a tangle of verbiage ... This is not a profession to be taken up

18. Anderson, M. D. Some personalities. *The Indexer* 7 (1) Spring 1970, 19-23

casually. Only a real student can hope to make a success of it; but to that privileged student the work is a delight. The art of dissecting sentences and paragraphs, of laying bare the thought behind the written word; the grouping together of allied headings and subordinate headings; the linking-up by cross-references; the critical editing and cutting down and out of every unnecessary entry; the joy of the final form – clear-cut, lucid, simple, and perfectly balanced – that is the true reward of the genuine worker. But it takes months of training, years of experience, before this happy result is attained.

However, not all the women who undertook to compile indexes were professionally trained or qualified to do so. John Thornton, a Vice-President of the Society of Indexers, complained in 1972, 'few indexes to medical and scientific books are adequate, and one suspects that many of them were compiled by the authors, their wives or secretaries, with no flair for the task'.[19] To this day, under most standard publishers' contracts, authors are responsible for providing indexes to their books: either by preparing them themselves, or by paying (part at least) of the fee for professional indexers. Sometimes the author's wife appears to have been appointed indexer *faute de mieux*, as the nearest person available at the moment the need is felt ('Darling, are you busy this week?'). An Open University Press sociology volume, *Women in Britain Today*, proclaimed in 1986:

> The work women do is not of course confined to housework ... some wives help their husbands in their occupations. The wives of publicans serve in the bar and make the sandwiches ... the wives of university lecturers proof-read and make indexes.

Sorry patronization sometimes results from tossing the indexing to the wife. Serious female indexers may wince at such printed acknowledgements as these examples from 1955 and 1984:

> The compilation of the index presented exceptional problems, and my wife took this burden from me. It is her only formal contribution to the volume, but all who write will know how much more important are the informal contributions of wives.

> I must also thank my wife Claudia for preparing the index (amongst other traditional wifely tasks).

The married state certainly need not preclude women from being competent indexers, but undertaking to love, honour and obey was

19. Thornton, John. The use of indexes. *The Indexer* 8 (1) April 1972, 17-19

not necessarily intended to include the indexing of the literary works of the master of the house. Indexing is not one of the domestic virtues.

The later 20th century brought true professionalism to indexing, with the foundation of the Society of Indexers (SI) in 1957, followed by affiliated societies in the US (1968), Australia (1976), and Canada (1977), and a British Standard on Indexing, first published in 1976. Then came the computer, often fallaciously credited with relieving indexers of the greater part, if not indeed the whole of their labours. Not at all: technology may ease and speed up the formerly manual processes of indexing, and the structural organization of an index, but can take no part in the determination of significance of references or the devising of linguistic terms to encapsulate and express them.

Computers are of more help in the compilation of indexes to dry, academic texts of specialist disciplines – scientific, technical, medical (STM) – and to manuals and instruction books, with their standardized terminology (often prescribed in paragraph headings) and formal structure, than to soft, humanities, narrative texts – stories of human lives as recounted in histories and biographies. Scientists read textbooks and STM journals to extract data and locate precisely defined concepts. The indexer of soft texts, by contrast, is often dealing with personal relationships and emotions, with recurrent or continuous themes rather than isolated facts, and has to make assessments as to the selection of items to index and the terms in which to express them on the basis of subjective value judgement. The indexer then becomes the interpreter, not just the reporter, of such texts.

Qualities of indexes

Indexes are necessary to readers who wish to know whether or not a publication holds information on the topics they seek, and if so, where exactly the references are to be found. The index, by nicely chosen subheadings, further specifies and differentiates what aspects are treated of, on which pages. It also brings together references that may be scattered through a book, and, by cross-references, indicates allied topics in the work.

Compiling indexes is skilled work, requiring qualities well beyond mere accuracy in recording page numbers and achieving alphabetical order. Indexers must use their judgement to decide which topics mentioned on a page might be sought by readers, and under what terms – including abstract concepts, not merely words that occur in the text. They must then devise terms to express them – perhaps generalizations for a series of names or minor topics – or conceptualise abstract notions and precis ideas or events to convey properly the concepts the index-user may expect to find. The resulting entries must then be arranged, as main headings, subheadings under main headings, sub-subs under the subheadings, in order: strictly alphabetical for the main headings, also alphabetical usually, or perhaps chronological, hierarchical, logical or classificatory for the subheadings. Synonymous terms must be combined, and cross-referred.

An essential quality for indexing is objectivity and freedom from bias. Attitudes are betrayed by choice of language, as well as by the degree of significance accorded to topics. Choice of terms is a great give-away, as in the famous conjugation, 'I practise fine economy / you are somewhat parsimonious / he is a right old skinflint'. Strong opinions may be expressed in the author's text, but the index should remain impartial, neither apparently endorsing nor contradicting them. However, indexing can offer a strong temptation to reflect or reinforce the tenets of the text – particularly for authors indexing their own work. 'After exhausting his weapons of attack in the preface, and in the body of the book, if he is very skilful a controversialist may let fly a few Parthian arrows from the Index', declared John Hill Burton in 1742.[20] *Brewer's Dictionary of Phrase and Fable* describes a Parthian shot as: 'a telling or wounding remark made on departure, giving one's adversary no time to reply. An allusion to the ancient practice of Parthian horsemen turning in flight, to discharge arrows and missiles at their pursuers'. Authors may thus seize the opportunity to further their cause in their own indexes, expanding there the attitudes and opinions already promulgated in the body of the book. A teacher may use the index didactically, even to the extent of duplicating or triplicating entries – on the snark-hunting Bellman's principle, 'what I tell you three times is true'.[21]

Likewise, there is danger in a strongly opinionated text's falling

20. John Hill Burton, *Book Hunter*, 1742
21. Piggott, Mary. Authors as their own indexers. *The Indexer* 17 (3) April 1991, 161-6

into the hands of an antagonist to compile its index, as Lord Macaulay recognized, insisting, when his eminently Whig history was published, 'Let no damned Tory index my book!'. Robert Collison observed, 'There have been several examples of books whose indexes, compiled by unscrupulous enemies, have been their ruin'.[22]

E.M. Hatt described the quality demanded of an indexer in this regard thus:

> If he is not impersonal, he is tactless ... Whatever the indexer's private convictions, he is not expected to prick bubbles and intrude opinions. He must not comment, judge or interpret (a *précis* is not a paraphrase). He sorts and summarizes, he mirrors and filters, but he has no colours on his palette.[23]

Excellent indexes may now receive proper recognition, be praised in reviews, nominated for awards – the Wheatley Medal annually presented for an outstanding index in the UK, the H. W. Wilson Award in the US. The extracts from indexes that follow – 57 actual published indexes to non-fiction; 14 examples of indexes to novels or verse; and 17 authors' portrayals of indexers in fiction – are presented not as model exemplars of their kind, but for particular curiosity value, for entertainment rather than use. They appeal in different ways: some from earlier centuries seem endearingly quaint; some amuse by their sheer badness; some are deliberately humorous, including parodies; some astonish by the vehemence of the views they present, even offering violent insult – these last mostly compiled by the authors of the works concerned.

Competence in indexing stems from skill in reading and writing – in analysing text and recognizing the most significant items, and the ability to express them in appropriate, concise terms. Then comes the structuring of the headings thus devised: a matter of conforming to established standards and rules. Guidance in indexing methods is found in the encyclopaedic *Indexing from A to Z* by Hans Wellisch (H. W. Wilson, 2nd edition 1995), and in *Indexing Books* by Nancy C. Mulvany (University of Chicago Press, 1994). A training course in five open learning units is offered by SI; details from Dept. 1, Society of Indexers, Globe Centre, Penistone Road, Sheffield S6 3AE. Book Indexing Postal Tutorials (BIPT) is

22. Collison, Robert. *Indexes and indexing.* 4th edition, Ernest Benn, 1972, 177
23. Hatt, E.M. Waxed parquets, worried bones. *The Indexer* 1 (1) March 1958, 14-16

a practical course of five tutorials with a manual on how to index; details from Ann Hall, The Lodge, Sidmount Avenue, Moffat, DG10 9BS. For authors indexing their own books, there is the 12-page *Indexing Your Book* by John Vickers (Society of Authors' Guide No. 13, 1996).

I became an indexer in 1965 – obviously, then, solely an indexer of printed works. Since then I have compiled some six hundred indexes to books and journals, but never ventured into the allied crafts of cataloguing, bibliography or electronic indexing for databases. This book refers only to the indexing of printed works.

As a professional indexer, I joined SI, and for 18 years, from 1978 to 1995, edited the journal it launched in 1958, *The Indexer*. We delighted in including there lighter items for their sheer entertainment or curiosity value. Readers sent many in, discovered in recherché old volumes, or comments on indexes noted in the press. I recently received a message, 'I miss seeing some of the entertaining articles and excerpts in *The Indexer*, since I got out of the information industry'. Many of the items presented in this collection are taken from issues of *The Indexer*. Authorship of comments and critiques not written by me is indicated by initials at the foot of those items; full details of the sources are given in the Acknowledgements on page 155.

The style of the original indexes is in general preserved here, in matters of typography and punctuation. Selected headings and subheadings are given, but with page numbers included only when there is special reason for this.

Hazel K. Bell

Life: not an index

To bring about order from chaos
   Is what indexers aim to achieve;
Reminiscent of God's first creation,
   Work mighty indeed to conceive.
I spend my days in the endeavour
   To impose whole correctness, no less;
All the text most efficiently signalled
   – Yet my desk's in a terrible mess.

Entries placed where each reader may seek them,
   Abstract concepts are all analysed
In elegant style, and with headings
   Precisely, concisely devised.
Cross-references all integrated
   In a model of intricateness;
Alphabeticization is flawless –
   So how come my house is a mess?

Deft structure of stratified headings
   To a nicety graded and ranked;
Hierarchy of neat indentations
   Wherein layers of meaning are banked.
If you asked, 'Is control here quite perfect?'
   I could answer with confidence, 'Yes';
All is accurate, clear and consistent –
   So why is my life such a mess?

Hazel K. Bell

INDEXES IN FACT

The proclaimed 'father of indexing', Henry B. Wheatley, laid down in 1902, 'One of the last things the genuine indexer thinks of is to make his work amusing'.[1] An indexer claimed in 1962, 'Conscious humour in indexing is rare, and rightly so, for it is almost indefensible. It is one of our tenets that the good index echoes the text in mood, texture, weight and substance. It follows that only a consciously humorous book should have a consciously humorous index ... index humour needs to be either an extension or a recasting of the lighthearted material it deals with.'[2] And Norman Knight, founder of the Society of Indexers, weighed in in 1979 with, 'Unconscious, or accidental, humour in an index is usually the result of bad indexing technique.'[3] Other inadvertent causes of humour in indexes are uncontrolled feelings of bias on the part of the indexer – whether or not they accord with those of the author – and the passage of time and change. The following extracts from indexes through the past centuries seem to me to give rise to great amusement, whether contrived or unconscious.

> *Though the idle deserve no crutches (let not a staff be used by them but on them), Pity it is the weary should be denied the benefit thereof, and industrious scholars prohibited the accommodation of an index.*
>
> Thomas Fuller (1608-61)

1. H. B. Wheatley, *How to Make an Index*. E. Stock, 1902
2. E. M. Hatt, 'Humour in indexing' *The Indexer* 3 (2), autumn 1962, 60-61
3. G. Norman Knight, *Indexing, the Art of*. Allen & Unwin, 1979, p. 182

Pre-19th century

: I :

The first printed index

The first printed index was appended to a tract by St Augustine, *De arte praedicandi* (On the art of preaching), a work very popular among 15th-century preachers, reprinted several times. It explained in elaborate detail how best to convey the message of a sermon to an audience. The anonymous editor and indexer says in his preface that he collated the text of several manuscripts from different places. The index is quite elaborate and sophisticated, with double entries, cross-references and even diagrammatic displays. The index entries were given as phrases, beginning with catchwords taken more or less verbatim from the text, and so rotated as to remain grammatically correct; for example (translated from the Latin original; alphabetized here in English):

Assent by listeners after the sermon, used to be done formerly
Alternation of voice in recitation
Goodwill of listeners, gaining of
It excites the mind of the listeners to speak and recite with ardour
Listeners, how to teach them
Study of the art of preaching, not to be neglected

The way of speaking excites, delights, influences, and moves ...
What is to be done by the faithful is not only to be taught but one ought to move and influence the listeners themselves towards such actions

H.H.W.

Index-learning turns no student pale,
Yet holds the eel of science by the tail.
Alexander Pope, *The Dunciad*, Book 1 (1728)

: 2 :

Quaintness is all

Robert Burton's *The Anatomy of Melancholy*, first completed in 1621, appears to be a medical work, but is described in the Tudor edition of 1927 by Floyd Dell and Paul Jordan-Smith (Tudor Publishing Company, New York) as 'a sort of literary cosmos, an omnium gatherum, a compendium of everything that caught the fancy of the scholar ... abounding in quaint conceits, excerpts and quotations'. The 52-page index to the 984-page text reflects this anecdotal profusion.

The prefatory note to the index includes, 'When other information is unavailable, Burton's own biographical and bibliographical remarks are sometimes given ... It is believed that the abbreviations will explain themselves.' The same insouciance is shown in some lists of page references, where the compiler has simply found it too tedious to assemble them all. The following entries all appear *sic*.

Biarmi, high priests who sanctify the wombs of the wives of the kings of Calicut, 856

Bilia, who took it for granted that all men had bad breaths like her husband (the story is St. Jerome's example of a truly modest wife), 853

Bulco Opiliensis, who did what he list, 927

Cabbage brings heaviness to the soul, 192

Calis, who would wash in no common water, 397

Climate, a cause of lust & jealousy, 827, 828

David 31, 32, 33, 47, 60, 113, 115, 156, 157, &c.

Devil the, 878, 938, &c.

Dibrenses, their strange aversion to unclean water, 907

Fish discommended, 192; defended, 398

Genesis, thought unadvisable reading, 771

Hart, a meat that hath an evil name, 190

Hilary's term (St Hilary's feast was in January; a term at Oxford and in the Eng. judicial sitting was named for it, but why Hilary's term should be proverbially hilarious does not appear), 252

Kisses, honest and otherwise, 701 et seq.

Non-natural things, the six, defined, 189

Nunnery, tricked by the Earl of Kent, 707

Pasquil (Pasquin was a bitter-tongued cobbler in 15th c.

At the laundress's at the Hole in the Wall in Cursitor's Alley up three pair of stairs ... you may speak to the gentleman, if his flux be over, who lies in the flock bed, my index maker.

Jonathan Swift,
Account of ... Mr Edmund Curll, Bookseller (1716)

Severest penalties incurred

William Prynne, 'an Utter-Barrister of Lincolnes Inn', lived 1600-69, and wrote and published many controversial Puritan pamphlets. In 1633 he published his *Histrio-Mastix: The Players Scourge*, which most rashly censured theatrical performances, so popular at the court of Charles I, and at a time when Queen Henrietta Maria herself was acting in a pastoral play. H.B. Wheatley observed (in *What is an Index?* 1878), 'The Index to Prynne's *Histrio-Mastix*, unlike the text, is very readable'.

Prynne's aspersions on thespians were emphasized in the 40-page index he himself prepared, as in the trenchant entry (abbreviated here):

> Women-Actors notorious whores ... and dare then any Christian women be so more than whorishly impudent as to act, to speake publikely on a stage perchance in man's apparell and cut haire here proved sinful and abominable in the presence of sundry men and women? ... O let such presidents of imprudency of impiety be never heard of or suffered among Christians, 385.

A further four pages are devoted to John Hooper, Bishop of Gloucester, who had been burned for heresy in 1555. The Bishop's sermons and letters are quoted at length. A sample entry is:

> Bishop Hooper preached twice every day of the weeke; would have Bishops to preach once every day, would have two sermons every Lord's Day, his censure of those who complain of too much preaching, 531.

Prynne was prosecuted in 1634 for impugning the virtue of Henrietta Maria, and the index was quoted at the trial by Attorney General Noy. Prynne was sentenced to have his book burnt by the hangman, pay a fine of £5000, be expelled from Oxford and Lincoln's Inn, to lose both ears in the pillory, and suffer perpetual imprisonment.

Questionable

John Dunton, an English bookseller, produced the successful *Athenian Gazette*, or *Casuistical Mercury* from 1691-97. This was a single half-sheet folio, published twice weekly and intended to resolve 'all the most nice and curious questions proposed by the ingenious'. Its indexes comprise one-line versions of the questions submitted to the Athenian Society, which at its largest seems to have comprised only Dunton himself, Richard Sault, John Norris and Samuel Wesley.

The index entries are arranged in first-letter alphabetical order by catchword, and within each letter are listed in the order of their publishing; for example:

> Hedg-hogs, how are they propagated? N. 6. q. 4
> Hist. of the *Ath. Society*, who writ it? N.10 q.1
> Head or feet, which travels most? N.10 9.9

As indexes they are unremarkable, being no more than a loosely ordered list of questions with no cross-referencing system. What is of interest is the persistence with which Dunton advertised his 'Alphabetical tables' and the reasons he offered for their usefulness. From the earliest issues, he draws his readers' attention to the finishing of each volume and each year's issues 'with a preface and index to the whole'. In the 'Supplement' to volume I, he enlarges on the index's use in a notice that is repeated in later volumes:

> ... at the end of every twelve months to draw up a general alphabetical table for the whole year, that so those gentlemen, or coffee-houses, that keep by them the several volumes, supplements, or single papers that are publisht from time to time may then bind them up all together, and by the help of the said ... table presently find any subject or question they have a mind to consult.

P.N.W.J.

: 5 :

One-man onslaught

In 1698 there erupted a right royal scholarly row. Charles Boyle, fourth Earl of Orrery, had edited and published the *Letters of Phalaris*. Dr Richard Bentley, in his *Dissertation on the Epistles of Phalaris*, showed these to be spurious. Boyle rose most indignantly to refute Bentley's charges, in a volume also titled *Dissertation on the Epistles of Phalaris*, followed by *examined By the Honourable Charles Boyle Esq*. In his preface he declared of Bentley, 'he is but a weak Champion in a very frivolous Cause ... He gave me so plain, and so publick an Affront, that I could not, with any tolerable regard to my reputation, quietly put it up'.

To the second edition of this book was added an index, by Dr William King. H. B. Wheatley, 'the father of indexing', wrote of this index, in the ninth edition of *The Encyclopaedia Britannica*, 1881, 'the witty Dr King was the first to use indexes as a method of attack'.

A trenchant attack indeed: a short index, with but two main headings, all the other entries being sub- and sub-subheadings, the whole rampant with sarcasm. We here transcribe it all.

A Short Account of
DR BENTLEY
By way of
INDEX

Dr Bentley's true story *of the MS prov'd false by the testimonies of*
— *Mr* Bennet.
— *Mr* Gibson.
— *Dr* King.
— *Dr* Bentley.
Dr Bentley's *civil usage of Mr* Boyle
His civil Language to
— *Mr* Boyle
— *Sir* W. Temple
His Singular Humanity to
— *Mr.* Boyle
— *Sir* Edward Sherburne
— *Foreigners*
His Ingenuity in
— *relating matters of fact*
— *citing authors*
— *transcribing and plundering Notes of and Prefaces of*
[five names given as sub-subheadings]
His Appeal to Foreigners
— *a Suspicious Plea*

— a false one
His charges against the
  Sophists return'd upon
  himself
— for forging History
— for Solacisms
— for egregious dulness
— for Pedantry
— for declaiming
His elegant Similes
His clean and gentile
  Metaphors
His nice taste
— in Wit
— in Stile and Language
— — in Greek
— — in Latin
— — in English
His old Sayings and Proverbs
His Collection of Asinine
  Proverbs, with an addition
His extraordinary talent at
  Drollery
His choice of weighty points
  to debate
His exactness in Chronology

His familiar acquaintance
  with Books that he never
  saw
His respect to the Bible
His New Discoveries
— of the Buda MS
— Empedocles's Epic Poem
His Old Discoveries ....
His dogmatic air
His modesty and decency in
  contradicting great men
— Plato
— [12 more names, and –
— all the moderns]
— Everybody
His happiness in confident
  assertions for want
— of Reading.
— of Judgment.
— of Sincerity
His Surprizing Consequences
His profound Skill in Criti-
  cism. From beginning to
  The End. [Sic, in place of
  page numbers!]

'Tis a pitiful piece of knowledge that can be learnt
from an index, and a poor ambition to be rich in the
inventory of another's treasure.

Joseph Glanvill, *The Vanity of Dogmatizing*, xv (1661)

: 6 :

Tory history – Whig indexer

When Lord Macaulay published his eminently Whig history, from 1848-61, he insisted, 'Let no damned Tory index my book!' A hundred years before, a Tory history had suffered a staunchly Whig index. The Tory historian was Archdeacon Laurence Echard (1670?-1730), the third volume of whose *History of England* was published in 1718. The Whig indexer was John Oldmixon (1673-1742), himself a historian, and author of poems and pamphlets against the Stuarts.

An anonymous pamphlet was published in 1729 about this example of bias in indexing. The title-page leads off in polemical style:

The
INDEX-WRITER
wherein
The Partiality and Disingenuity of
the Worthy Author of the *Critical
History of England*, the *Secret History
of Europe*, and his last famous Work,
Entitled, *The History of England, under
the Respective Reigns of the Royal
Family of Stuarts,* are fully exposed.
AND
Divers Historical Facts set in a true Light, and rescued from
the Misrepresentations of that WHIG HISTORIAN.

The Lie *no true bred* Whig *cou'd ever balk*;
Lies *are the Strength & Substance of their Talk*
Expede Herculem.

London: *Printed for* J. Wilford, *near* Stationers Hall.
MDCCXXIX.
Price 4d.

After the title-page follows the Advertisement, calculated to puncture the prestige of indexers by its reference to their 'low employment':

ADVERTISEMENT

It may not be amiss to acquaint the Reader, that when Mr. Arch-Deacon Echard had finished his 3d Vol. of the History of England, the Drudgery of compiling an Index, was left to one who was thought not unfit for so low an Employment as giving an Alphabetical Epitome of that Volume: It was not suspected that one thus Employ'd should be so utterly void of all Shame as to pervert the meaning of his Author, where the Abuse might be so easily discovered, and his unfairness laid open to publick View: But it has so happen'd that the strong Propension this Person had to serve the Whig faction, and the little Regard he bore to Truth, put him upon framing an Index, in many Places, contrary to the History, which the Reader will, to his Surprize, find giving one Account, and the Index another: This unfair Practice is the Subject of the following Tract.

The tract itself opens with yet another piece of invective:

The Compiler of the *Index* to the 3d Vol. of Mr Arch-Deacon *Echard's* History of *England*, might have gone on untaken notice of, in a publick way, and disregarded, had he confin'd his Partiality, and Unfairness to writing of *Indexes*; where he could only have shewn an Inclination to Mischief, without Ability to Effect it; and where the Antidote would have been still Ready to prevent the fatal Effects of the Poyson. But as the Piper is turned Lutanist, and the Index-writer has quitted that humble Task, and Display'd his Talents in History, and may, under the Character of an Historian, by his bold and confident way of Writing impose on the unwary and Credulous, and that the Infamy of the present Age, may not pass for History in the next, 'tis fit the World should know how well Qualified (in point of Candor, and Ingenuity) this Misrepresenter of Facts, is to write Critical and Secret History. To put the Reader then upon his Guard against the Fraud, and Craft of a dangerous Adversary, who lies in wait to deceive, and that this Man of Art may appear in his true Shape, and proper Colours, I shall select some Instances of this Gentleman's slight of Hand, in this lesser Work, that when the Reader comes to his Grand Performances, and reads over his Historical Collections, He may not give himself up entirely to the Conduct of a false Guide, may not always take bold Allegations for undoubted Facts, nor receive for evident Truths whatever shall with great Assurance be affirmed, but subject the Works of a suspected Author, to a strict Enquiry and close Examination, and having in constant View the Tricks of the Index-writer, may the better secure himself against the Impositions of the Historian.

Having got his reader into an appropriate frame of mind, the pamphleteer then gives quotations from Echard's text, with the corresponding index entries, and copious comments. A selection follows:

To begin, "Shortly after, says Mr. *Echard*, *Richard Nelthorp*, together with *John Ayloff*, were brought from Newgate to the King's-Bench-Bar; where being ask'd, Why Execution should not be awarded against them, in regard they stood attainted by Outlawry of High Treason, for conspiring the Death of King *Charles* the II and having nothing to say that could avail them, the Court made a Rule that they should both be Executed the *Friday* following, and accordingly they were then hang'd, Mr. *Nelthorp*, before *Gray's-Inn* in *Holborn*, and Mr. *Ayloff*, before the *Temple Gate* in *Fleet-street*."

The Index Thus "*Nelthorp, Richard*, a Lawyer, hang'd without Tryal in King *James's* Time". And in another Place, "*Ayloff, John*, hang'd without a Tryal in King *James's* Reign." I dont here charge the *Index-writer* with saying what is in Terms false, but for suppressing the true Cause of their being hang'd without Tryal, *viz.* That they stood attainted by Outlawry, and on that Account had by Law forfeited all Right and Title to it. The Industrious concealing whereof, is manifestly from a malicious Design to cast an Odium on that Reign, by representing the Prince as a Murderer of his Subjects ...

Mr. *Echard* having Occasion to speak of some things publish'd in a secret History, intimates his disbelief thereof, in these Words, "But of this, and the Letters said to have pass'd between *Monmouth*, and *Albemarle*, we have not all the Certainty that is requisite to an History that is not Secret." Which the *Index-writer* (according to his usual Candour) renders thus, "Histories, secret, dont require much Certainty." Thus does the Author lie at the Mercy of a Man, who makes no Conscience, to Alter, Disguise, Diminish, or Add, as best suited his Purpose ...

Echard, "*Shaftsbury* removed his Lodgings into *Wapping*, the very Night that Place was Burnt, being the *Night of the same 19th of November*, when he expected to set the Nation on a Flame, privately sculk'd down the River, and took Shipping for *Holland*; leaving his Friends with this Ominous Prognostick, *that the Design could not long be conceal'd*, there being so many acquainted with it. Which proved true, tho' he did not live to see it fulfill'd. And of the 30 Agents formerly mention'd, eight, *viz.* Lord *Howard*, *Romsey*, *Sheppard*, *West*, *Kealing*, *Brown*, *Lea*, and *Barbar*, all afterwards turn'd Discoverers and Informers." *Index*, "Informers eight notable ones." Now methinks *Shaftsbury's* precipitate *Flight* out of Fear of a sudden Discovery, or a Prognostick of *Shaftsbury* verified; would have better deserved a place in the Index, as conveying the principal Ideas of the forecited Passage; But the giving the true sense of the Author, seems by this Epitome to have been the least Part of the *Index-writer's* Design; inclined rather by this Contemptuous Expression to disparage and bring into Disrepute the Discoverers of the Fanatick Conspiracy, and in order to discredit the Information, to mark the Informers *Nigro Carbone*. I'll for once put a Case, suppose the Printer of that renown'd Piece call'd the *Secret History of Europe*, should have taken upon him to add to that Title these *Words, Wrote by a notable Person*, and subjoin'd this memorable saying for a Motto, *Secret Histories dont require much Certainty*. It would not be hard to guess at the worthy Author's Thoughts in that Case, how he would have liked that Liberty, and by what Name called that Treatment ...

Echard, "Next they tell us, the means whereby they resolved to accomplish this vast Undertaking, by Killing the King. As first, *Grove* and *Pickering* to Shoot him. Secondly, *Conyers* and *Anderton*, two Benedictine Monks, and four Irish Ruffians to stab him, and Thirdly "*Sir George Wakeman*, the Queen's Physician to Poison him." *Index*, "*Wakeman* (Sir *George*) Physician to King *Charles* the II undertakes to Poison him." Now what is here so positively asserted in the *Index*, as if it were a matter evident and past all doubt, and contradiction is in the Body of the History barely mention'd, as a part of Oates's Narrative, a material Difference and may serve as another Instance of the unfairness and partiality of the *Index-writer*.

Echard, "As to the Warming pan, it was reply'd, that it had been impossible to put a New-born Child, *cum secundinis*, in the narrow Compass of a Warming-pan without stifling it." *Index*, "Warming-pan, very useful to King *James's* Queen." Now here the Fellow sneers at a Lady of sublime Quality, and at the same time ridicules his Author; and tho' this envenom'd Writer had no regard to Majesty, one would think, as an hireling, he might have shewn some to the Person who paid him: And if his Master, in so large a work, where Sleep is apt to surprise the most Watchful, had happened to have said a weak thing, it ill became him to expose him, but it so falls out, that this Saying of Mr. *Echard*, "that it had been impossible to have put a New-born Child, *cum Secundinis*, into so narrow a Compass, without stifling it," is far from being ridiculous, when 'tis considered that a Warming-pan is usually about 7 inches or 7 and a half over, and a New-born Child in Length about 16 Inches ...

Echard, "Also Mr. *Wilmore*, the Foreman of *Stephen College's Ignoramus Jury*, having convey'd away a young Boy, and sent him to *Jamaica*, a Writ *de Homine Replegiando* was brought against him, upon which the Sheriffs, *Pilkington* and *Shute* made an insufficient return and positively refused to return *Elongatus est*, the only legal return in that Case. They were both brought to the King's-Bench-Bar upon an Attachment, where they received a sharp Reprimand from the Court, and were glad to submit with a Promise of better Behaviour for the Future. Hereupon an *Elongatus est* being returned, a *Capias in Withernam* issued out against *Wilmore*, to take him into Custody till he had produced the Boy. Nor was this sufficient but the said *Wilmore*, was at the End of May Tryed at the King's-Bench upon an Information exhibited against him by the Attorney General, for Kidnapping the said Boy, being under the Age of 13, and unknown to his Parents; and upon full Evidence of the plain Fact, he was found Guilty by a Kentish Jury, who never went from the Bar." *Index*, "*Wilmore* prosecuted Maliciously." As this story gives a pretty lively Image of the Faction, it will bear being considered Circumstantially, and may serve as a Picture of a true Protestant of those Times. The Behaviour of the Sheriffs is highly culpable, as they prostituted their Authority to a vile and scandalous Purpose, to stop a legal Prosecution of a very Notorious Offender, upon an Unwarrantable Motive, for his having served the Party in a Dishonourable way, and to the Encouragement of Villainy in such as should Espouse their Cause. The Action of the Criminal, which was *Boy-stealing* is so flagitious and detestable, that the bare mention thereof sufficiently exposes its baseness and Turpitude. The part the *London* Grand-Jury acted in Skreening this Offender by an *Ignoramus*, is Infamous enough, and shews what slight hold Oaths had taken of the Consciences of these true blue Protestants, when they judged their Cause might be promoted by Perjury. These Crimes of *Wilmore*, the Sheriffs and the Grand-Jury are untaken Notice of in the Index, which instead of pointing out these vile Practices, endeavours to mislead the Reader into an Opinion of the Innocence of the Criminal, who is there said, contrary to all Truth, to be *Maliciously Prosecuted*. When therefore such an *Index-writer* shall set up for a Discoverer of Secrets, for profound skill in History, and shall have the presumption, *per Honestas Ire Domos*. Then 'tis most necessary for the Reader to guard himself against all his Artifices and design'd Impositions, following this advice of *Horace*

Hunc tu Romane Caveto.

FINIS

M.D.A.

Doctor Nonentity, a metaphysician ... Most people think him a profound scholar: but as he seldom speaks, I cannot be positive in that particular. He generally spreads himself before the fire, folds his hands, talks little, drinks much ... I am told he writes indexes to perfection.

Oliver Goldsmith,
The Citizen of The World, letter no. 7 (1759)

: 7 :

Can it be so?

Cross-references from the index to *A Treatise of the Pleas of the Crown* (or 'A SYSTEM of the Principal Matters relating to that SUBJECT, digefted under their proper Heads') (1724) attributed to William Hawkins, Serjeant at Law, suggest sometimes sheer surrealism, sometimes deep pessimism. The imprint reads: 'London: Printed by the Affigns of E. SAYER, Efq; for J. WALTHOE in the *Middle-Temple-Cloyfters*. MDCCXXIV.'

Cattle *see* Clergy.	Honour *see* Constable.
Chastity *see* Homicide.	Incapacity *see* Officers.
Coin *see* High Treason.	King *see* Treason.
Convicts *see* Clergy.	Knaves *see* Words.
Death *see* Appeal.	Letters *see* Libel.
Election *see* Bribery.	London *see* Outlawry.
Fear *see* Robbery.	Shop *see* Burglary.

: 8 :

All in the family

Roger North, in his own history of his family, *The Lives of the Norths*, published 1742-44, shows mighty nepotism in indicating the text under the heading for one of his brothers:

NORTH, FRANCIS:
Mr North modest to a weakness;
His skill in the law inferior to none;
never guilty of an error to his disadvantage;
General scholar and virtuoso ...
His inclinations always to loyalty;
Never retrograde;
Allowed to be a good judge even by his enemies;
His affability and patience

: 9 :

For the fair sex

The *Lady's Magazine or Entertaining Companion for the Fair Sex* is
described on its title page as 'Appropriated Solely to their Use and
Amusement' (printed for G. Robinson, Paternoster Row, London).

Its indexes show signs of similar adaptation for the gentle ears.
There is much food for thought in their 1742 INDEX TO THE
DEBATES IN THE POLITICAL CLUB, TO THE ESSAYS,
POLITICS, DOMESTICK AND FOREIGN OCCURRENCES
&c.:

Beauty, the Power of, and the
Influence the fair Sex might
have in reforming the Manners of the World

Burials, Monthly Account of,
[two lines of page refer-
ences]. Yearly account of 632

Charles I. a good story of him.
The Case in his Reign. Original Cause of his Ruin

Christnings. *See* Burials

Dream of a bad fallen Minister

Evidence, the Method of
procuring it by promising a
pardon or Reward, found
fault with

Europe, to what the present
unhappy State of its Affairs
is owing

Fair Sex. *See* Beauty

Free Governments, the Incon-
veniences objected to them
answer'd

Free People must be treated
like a fine Woman

Greeks and Romans, the Honours paid to their great Men
and publick Benefactors,
compar'd with the Treat-
ment some modern States-
men have met with

Insect, aquatick, a remarkable
one

Ladies, their Power over their
Lovers, and their Influence
over their Posterity

The entries from the 'INDEX TO THE ESSAYS, LETTERS,
and other Pieces in PROSE' to Vol. VII, for 1776 are even more
deliberately addressed to their market.

Dress, ladies, for March
thoughts on it

Dullness, humorously
described

Essays on several subjects, particularly addressed to the fair
sex

Fair Sex, effusions in praise of
them

The most accomplished way of using books at present is twofold: either, first, to serve them as men do lords – learn their titles exactly and then brag of their acquaintance; or, secondly, which is, indeed, the choicer, the profounder and politer method, to get a thorough insight into the index, by which the whole book is governed and turned, like fishes by the tail. For to enter the palace of learning at the great gate requires an expense of time and forms, therefore men of much haste and little ceremony are content to get in by the back door.

Jonathan Swift, *A Tale of a Tub* (1701)

: 10 :

Nature notes with footnote

In a letter to his friend Samuel Barker, on 8 January 1788, the Selborne naturalist, Gilbert White, wrote:

> I have been very busy of late; and have at length put my last hand to my Natural History and Antiquities of the parish. However, I am still employed in making an Index; an occupation full as entertaining as that of darning stockings, though by no means so advantageous to society. My work will be well got up, with a good type, and on good paper; and will be embellished with several engravings.
>
> It is remarkable enough that there is now sitting at my elbow an Oxford gentleman (the rev. R. Churton) who is deeply employed in making an Index also: so that my old parlor is become quite an *Index manufactory*.

Here are some of the charming entries from White's *History of Selborne*, published by Benjamin White & Son in 1789 – an index complete with its own footnote.

ANNE, Queen, came to *Wolmer-forest* to see the red deer
April, 1770, the remarkable inclemency of the weather
Ash-tree, a rupture one, what
_____ a shrew one, what
August, the most mute month respecting the singing of birds
Black-cap, an elegant songster
Castration, its strange effects
Cats, house, strange that they should be so fond of fish
Crocus, the spring, and saffron, their different seasons of blossoming, wonderful, why
Daws breed in unlikely places
Dispersion of birds, pretty equal, why
Fishes, gold and silver, why very amusing in a glass bowl
Fly, bacon, injurious to the housewife
Frogs, migrate from pools
Hogs, would live, if suffered, to a considerable age
Rooks, perfectly white
_____ an amusing anecdote about
Slugs,* very injurious to wheat just come out of the ground, by eating

* For the amazing ravages committed on turnips, wheat, clover, field cabbage-seeds, &c. by *slugs*, and a rational and easy method of destroying them, see a sensible letter by Mr. *Henry Vogg*, of *Chilcompton*, in the county of *Somerset*, lately made public at the request of the gentlemen of that neighbourhood.

off the blade; and by their infinite numbers occasioning incredible havock

Snake, stinks *se defendendo*

Sow, prodigious fecundity of one

Tortoise, a family one

_____ more particulars of

_____ farther circumstances about

Worms, earth, no inconsiderable link in the chain of nature, some account of

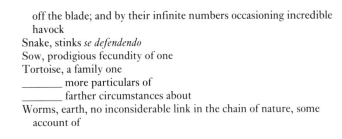

[The] modern device of consulting indexes ... is to read books Hebraically, and begin where others usually end.

Jonathan Swift, *A Letter of Advice to a Young Poet* (1720)

19th century

Blackmail

The *Memoirs ... and Amatory Anecdotes of Illustrious Persons* of the Regency courtesan, Harriette Wilson, were first published (by John Joseph Stockdale) in instalments in 1825. The publication was financed by the ingenious method of writing to various people whose names figured in the book, telling them that they would find themselves unmercifully quizzed in a forthcoming work by Miss Wilson, and suggesting that a cash payment would 'prevent unpleasantness'. At the end of each published part appeared an advertisement of the names of the people to be mentioned in the next number, thus giving them another chance of buying themselves off.

The memoirs enjoyed a *succés de scandale*. Thirty-five 'editions' were produced in a year; they were translated and appeared in Paris, Brussels and Stuttgart, and serialised in *Bell's Life in London*. There were libel suits. In 1831 Stockdale brought out a new edition of the *Memoirs*, incorporating previously unpublished parts. The index to this edition fills more than a volume and a half, and, according to Angela Thirkell, Wilson's 20th-century biographer, 'leaves nothing to the imagination. A few extracts will show its range'. She quotes entries, *sic*:

ADULTERY. Insufferable, by anyone not of royal blood, except in private, like Lords Cowper and Marlborough.
MUTTON. A hot leg of, thrown by Lord Berwick at the footman.
STOCKDALE, JB (*this is master Stockdale Junior, the 'Miah' of the prosecution*).
　　Notices the appropriateness of the psalms.
　　Considerateness of.
　　Has lost a glorious opportunity.
　　Contrasted with jews.

A century later, Angela Thirkell's *The Fortunes of Harriette*, a biography of Harriette Wilson, based on Wilson's original *Memoirs*, was published by Hamish Hamilton in 1936. The index to Thirkell's book includes these further enlightening entries:

: 12 :

Thinking it over

The 67-page index to William Pickering's three-volume 1835 edition of *The Works of Sir Thomas Browne*, edited by Simon Wilkin, has a chatty tone, inducing one to wish to read the text – though, one wonders, could one learn any more from the original pages thus fully indicated?

ARISTOTLE: generally supposed that he drowned himself in Euripus because he could not explain its flux and reflux, 332; most improbable, 333

ELEPHANT: how his knees bend, 215; that he hath no joints, 385, that he's terrified by the grunting of swine, 295

EAR: horse leech in, remedy for, 233; tingling of, ominous, 165

HARES, RABBITS: none in Iceland, 22; and cabbage, Cato's chief diet, 510

: 13 :
Awful fates of authors

Isaac D'Israeli, English man of letters and father of statesman Benjamin Disraeli, wrote more than 20 books. André Maurois puts it (in *Disraeli*, D. Appleton and Company, 1928), 'In the beginning the goal of this labour was the writing of a *History of English Literature*. But ... D'Israeli found himself overwhelmed by a rising tide of paper slips, and resigned himself to the humble but diverting function of a compiler. ... he published a collection of anecdotes which enjoyed great success and decided his career.' His forte was in literary illustrations of persons and history, as in his collections of essays: *Amenities of Literature, Curiosities of Literature, Quarrels of Authors* and *Calamities of Authors*. This last was stated by its publishers, Frederick Warne and Co., to comprise 'a diversified miscellany of literary, artistic and political history, of critical disquisition and biographic anecdote'. The 1840 edition included an index from which the following entries are taken, indicating calamities of authors indeed.

Authors, Horace Walpole affects to despise them
——their maladies
——case of, stated
——incompetent remuneration of
——who wrote above the genius of their own age
——ill reception from the public of their valuable works
——who have sacrificed their fortunes to their studies, *ib.*
——who commenced their literary life with ardour, and found their genius obstructed by numerous causes,
——who have never published their works
——provincial, liable to bad passions

——by profession, a phrase of modern origin
——original letter to a minister from one
——Fielding's apology for them
Barnes, Joshua, his pathetic letter descriptive of his literary calamities
Bayne, Alexander, dies of intense application
Booksellers in the reign of Elizabeth
——why their interest is rarely combined with the advancement of literature
——why they prefer the crude to the matured fruit
Carey, Henry, author of several of our national poems ... his miserable end

Castell, Dr., ruined in health and fortune by the publication of his Polyglott

Churchyard, Thomas, his pathetic description of his wretched old age

Cotgrave, Randle, falls blind in the labour of his Dictionary

Critic, poetical, without any taste, how he contrived to criticise poems

Criticism, illiberal, some of its consequences stated

Drake, Dr. John, a political writer, his miserable life

Drayton's national work, the Polyolbion, ill received, and the author greatly dejected

Greene, Robert, a town wit, his poverty and death

Henry, Dr., the Historian, the sale of his work, on which he had expended most of his fortune and his life, stopped, and himself ridiculed by a conspiracy raised against him

Heron, Robert, draws up the distresses of a man of letters living by literary industry, in the confinement of a sponging-house, from his original letter

Howel, nearly lost his life by excessive study

Hume, his literary life how mortified with disappointments

Kenrick, Dr., a caustic critic, treats our great authors with the most amusing arrogance

Logan, ... dies broken-hearted

Macdiarmid, John, died of over-study and exhaustion

Milton's works the favourite prey of booksellers

Ockley, Simon, exults in prison for the leisure it affords for study

Poets, mediocre Critics are the real origin of mediocre

Prynne, a voluminous author without judgement, but the character of the man not so ridiculous as the author; seldom dined

Ritson, Joseph, the late poetical antiquary, carried criticism to insanity

Ritson, Isaac, a young Scotch writer, perishes by attempting to exist by the efforts of his pen

Steele, his ill choice in a wife of an uncongenial character

Subscriptions once inundated our literature with worthless work

Walpole, Horace, his literary mortifications ...

Kevin Jackson comments (in *Invisible Forms*, 1999), 'An enlightened Arts Council would have this index reprinted in pamphlet form and issued gratis to any young person contemplating a career as an *homme* or *femme de lettres*'.

Robust pamphleteering

In 1850 Thomas Carlyle wrote what he called 'a set of Reform Discourses', eight pamphlets entitled *The Present Time, Model Prisons, Downing Street, The New Downing Street, Stump Orator, Parliaments, Hudson's Statue*, and *Jesuitism*. They were regarded as ferocious, pessimistic, callous and bigoted, showing a loathing of contemporary attitudes. They were first published separately, then in a single volume by Chapman and Hall in The Shilling Edition of Thomas Carlyle's Works. No date is given for the volume, and there is no credit for the indexer, but the volume is 'edited by Thomas Carlyle', who was working on it in 1857.

: 15 :

Some have greatness thrust upon them

A possibly apocryphal entry, first quoted by Leigh Hunt in *The Examiner*, which he and his brother ran from 1808 to 1825, is reputed to appear in a lawbook referring to the comment of Sir William Draper Best, a Puisne Judge of the King's bench, that he had 'a great mind to commit the man for trial'. This is said to appear in the index as:

Best (Mr. Justice), his great mind

Enhancing the text

John Ruskin addressed a series of papers, *Fors Clavigera*, 'To the Workmen and Labourers of Great Britain', from 1871-84, in which he discussed his social philosophy. The letters were published monthly and sold at 7 pence each through Ruskin's agent, George Allen, of Keston, Kent. Ruskin himself indexed the eight volumes published by Allen, 1873-95. He makes use of his indexes in a most engaging way to supply comments on, or corrections to, his original text. We present here an extract from the index to the letters for 1871-72, preserving exactly the style of the original, the volume number in bold followed by the page numbers in roman.

The entry for 'Bakewell and Buxton' refers to this passage in the text, protesting about the railway built through the gorge of the Wye in Derbyshire:

> The valley is gone, and the Gods with it, and now, every fool in Buxton can be at Bakewell in half an hour, and every fool in Bakewell at Buxton; which you think a lucrative process of exchange—you Fools Everywhere.

Army, the English, according to Mr. Grant Duff, of no use, **15**, 10; standing, function of, under type of scarecrow, **11**, 9. In that passage I ought to have indicated the function of the quiet scarecrow as that of keeping order in one's fields;—compare **2**, 14, at bottom of page, and passage on Horse Guards, **19**, 5; the parallel domestic *mischief* is described in **8**, 9.

Art, the author's practical work in **9**, 19; laws of its greatness, **9**, 20; worst thing conceivably produceable by, at Kensington, 5, 6; Kensington system of teaching, **9**, 19, its relations to science, – no one can live by the fine arts, **1**, 13.

Artists are included under the term workmen, **11**, 10, but I see the passage is inaccurate, – for I of course meant to include musicians among artists, and therefore among working men; but musicians are not 'developments of tailor or carpenter.' Also it may be questioned why I do not count the work given to construct poetry, when I count that given to perform music, this will be explained in another place.

Author of this book, his given duty, **1**, 5; his political indefinableness, **1**, 7; his early life, **10**, 7, **24**, 6.

Badness (see Goodness).

Bakewell and Buxton, how reciprocally advantaged by railway, **5**, 12.

Bedford, Duke of, his costly purchase, **4**, 12.

Benevolent persons, the fatallest mistake of, **9**, 6.

Birmingham *Morning News,* extract from letter in, **11**, 15; singular letter from resident at, **6**, 9.

Bismarck, Count, had little to do with German War, **3**, 5.

Boilers, steam, the gods of the modern, **14**, 22.

Bombay, question as to importance of first telegraphic message to, **5**, 11.

Bookselling, author's principles of, **6**, 6, 11, 19, and see correspondence at end of **14** and **15**.

Bread, Christian life begins in breaking, **12**, 26; English lawyer's speech concerning, **12**, 14.

Brown, Mr. Rawdon, his work on the English in Italy, **1**, 9, **15**, 12 (note), where please insert comma after 'translation.'

Bullion, its influx does not enrich the country, **22**, 8.

Buxton (see Bakewell).

Candles, pious expenditure of in France, **6**, 16.

Capital, the small importance of, to industry, **1**, 16; Mr. Mill's mode of increasing, **2**, 8; compare **1**, 12; Mr. Fawcett's account of, **11**, 11; is properly represented by the general type of carpenter's plane, and must not therefore be borrowed, **11**, 10; see **22**, 13.

Carlyle: highly esteems force, **13**, 4, 8; his teaching of the nature law, **10**, 19; abuse of him by fools, **10**, 20.

Castles, advantage of England over America in the possession of them, **10**, 9; strongholds of injustice, **10**, 18; internal police of, 10, 17.

Chapelle, Sainte, of Paris, how mischievous to France, **3**, 10; danger of, in revolution of 1871, **6**, 18.

J.A.V.

A full index is added, without which no publication beyond the size of a pamphlet can be deemed compleat.

John Northcouck,
Preface to Grand Lodge Book of Constitutions (1784)

Prominence of inessentials

Samuel Palmer compiled a regular index to *The Times* in the 19th century, his first volume appearing in 1868, back numbers being subsequently indexed. Economy was a prime necessity: two or more entries per news item were unallowable luxuries, and cross-references were also at a premium; the rule seems to have been one entry per news item. But Palmer's method of choosing subject headings was, to say the least, eccentric. These are typical examples from the volume for October-December 1842.

The first relates to a floating chapel which was loosed from its moorings on the River Severn; it is indexed under the heading *Disgraceful Act*. When referring to the dry weather they were experiencing that year the entry is *Present Dry Season*, but there are also references on the same subject under 'Weather'.

Two women were committed to Ruthin prison, one, named Amelia House, for firing a pistol at a man called Roberts; the other, named Jane Williams, for stealing a mare belonging to a Robert Owen. These escapades are indexed to *Rather uncommon for females*. A storm in France is under *Fatal Storm*, and a small boy sentenced for stealing a twopenny pie goes to *Atrocious Criminal*.

But in view of the need for economy, Palmer did not always keep his references short and to the point. The case of a certain Jane Thomas, who apparently was so overcome with joy at seeing her mother at the stage door that she died in her arms, reads thus:

> 'Death of Jane Thomas in her Mother's Arms in Holborn at Joy in Seeing her parent at the Stage Door to Receive her.'

C.H.J.K.

Erotic pedantry – or pedantic eroticism?

Henry Spencer Ashbee was a Victorian bibliographer who enthusi-astically collected pornography, and earnestly catalogued his entire collection. He published his *Index Librorum Prohibitorum* ('Index of Books Worthy of Being Prohibited'), in a limited edition, in 1877. Ian Gibson devotes an entire chapter of his biography of Ashbee, *The Erotomaniac* (Faber & Faber, 2001), to this book, deeming it 'One of the most deliberately subversive works ever written in the English language'.

The volume made 544 pages, in 'a handsome array of different typefaces and decorative fleurons', 'sumptuously bound'. It inclu-ded a 68-page introduction (with 1400 footnotes), 436 pages of bibliography devoted to some 150 books in six languages, 38 pages of 'Authorities Consulted', illustrative plates, and a 'General, Alphabetical and Analytical Index' of 58 pages in two columns. This index was exhaustive, including authors (listed in small capi-tals), publishers, titles (such as 'Miss Bellasis Birched for Thiev-ing' and 'The Marchioness' Amorous Pastimes', in Old English typeface), names of characters in the books, and subjects treated (in Antique type). Gibson describes it as 'An earnest of [Ashbee's] obsessive need to classify, arrange, order and pin down'. Here are some specimen entries.

> BACKSIDES can blush, 352
> BIBLIOGRAPHY. [A nine-column entry, including the subheadings –]
>   English writers and artists (erotic) inferior to Foreigners, xviii
>   No satisfactory catalogue of erotic literature exists, xvi
>   The more a book is prohibited the more it is sought, xxvi.
>   Obscene words used, but only when unavoidable, lxviii.
>   Obscenity is in the mind, not in words, lxviii (note 110).
> COPULATION. [many subheadings, including] –
>   Monotony condemned.
>   Preliminaries described.
>   The two most natural modes are the best.
>   Various postures enumerated.
>   A woman may be enjoyed by two men at the same time.
>   The woman should not be quite naked.

Racy and racist

The Biglow Papers, by the American poet and diplomat James Russell Lowell, was published in 1886 by the American poet and diplomatist George Routledge (and Sons). It consists of satirical prose and verse of the period of the American war with Mexico (1846-48) and the American civil war (1861-65), written partly in the Yankee dialect.

The 1886 edition has two series each of eleven papers (poems, purported letters and speeches), each preceded by a lengthy introduction and reviews, followed by a five-page glossary and 35-page 'copious index' (so described on the title page). It is most thoroughly both racy and racist.

Here is a sample of the glossary:

Wannut, *walnut (hickory)*.
Ware, *where*.
Ware, *were*.
Whopper, *an uncommonly large lie*; as, that General Taylor is in favour of the Wilmot Proviso.
Wig, *Whig*; a party now dissolved.

Wunt, *will not*.
Wus, *worse*.
Wut, *what*.
Wuth, *worth*; as *Antislavery Perfessions 'fore 'lection ain't wuth a Bungtown copper*.
Wuz, *was*, sometimes were.

These are some extracts from the index:

Babel, probably the first Congress, 82 – a gabble-mill, *ib.*
Bagowind, Hon. Mr., whether to be damned, 89
Birch, virtue of, in instilling certain of the dead languages, 114
Bonaparte, N., a usurper, 103
Bonds, Confederate, their specie-basis cutlery, 207—when payable, (attention, British stockholders!) 268
Boston, people of, supposed educated, 59, note—has a good opinion of itself, 226
Ham, sandwich, an orthodox (but

peculiar) one, 89—his seed, 248—their privilege in the Bible, *ib.*—immoral justification of, 249
Hotels, big ones, humbugs, 234
Journals, British, their brutal tone, 217
Mill, Stuart, his low ideas, 269
Russell, Earl, is good enough to expound our Constitution for us, 218
Shot at sight, privilege of being, 253
Store, cheap cash, a wicked fraud, 115

Some items, far indeed from political correctness, may give offence to modern eyes. Can they be held examples of improper bias in indexing, when they faithfully reflect the deliberately sardonic parodies of the text? We quote some such below, with apologies, each entry followed by the lines of text to which it refers.

Bible, not composed for use of coloured persons, 248
(*Text runs*: Ain't it belittlin' the Good Book in all it's proudes' featurs
To think 'twuz wrote for black an' brown an' 'lasses-coloured creaturs?)

Coloured folks, curious national diversion of kicking, 60
(*Text runs*: I'd an idee thet they were built arter the darkie fashion all,
An' kickin' colored folks about, you know, 's a kind o' national)

Coon, old, pleasure in skinning, 86
(*Text runs*: "Yes," sez Davis o' Miss, "The perfection o' bliss,
Is in skinnin' thet same old coon," sez he.)

Mexicans charged with various breaches of etiquette, 60—kind feelings beaten into them, 94
(*Text runs*: The Mex'cans don't fight fair, they say, they piz'n all the water,
An' du amazin' lots of things thet isn't wut they ough' to)
(I du believe wutever trash
'll keep the people in blindeness,—
Thet we the Mexicuns can thrash
Right inter brotherly kindness)

Niggers, area of abusing, extended, 76—Mr. Sawin's opinion of, 125
(*Text runs*: Ez fer Mexico, 'tain't no great glory to lick it,
But 'twould be a darned shame to go pullin' o' triggers
To extend the aree of abusin' the niggers.)
(Ez fer the niggers, I've ben South, an' thet hez changed my min';
A lazier, more ungrateful set, you couldn't nowers fin'.)

Domestic plus moral guidance

The single-volume domestic encyclopaedia, *Enquire Within upon Everything* (78th edition, revised, published by Houlston & Sons in 1888), offers guidance on all matters 'provided your desire has relations to the necessities of domestic life'. It is furnished with a 27-page, triple-column index to its 388 pages (numbers in the index referring to the paragraphs, not the pages). The editor (whose name seems not to be given) boasts in his preface:

> IF there be any among my Readers who, having turned over the pages of "Enquire Within" have hastily pronounced them to be confused and ill-arranged, let them at once refer to THE INDEX, at page 389, and for ever hold their peace. THE INDEX is, to the vast congregation of useful hints and recipes that fill the pages of this volume, what the DIRECTORY is to the great aggregation of houses and people in London.

Then he most fancifully extends his metaphor:

> No one, being a stranger to London, would run about asking for "MR. Smith". But, remembering the Christian name and the profession of the individual wanted, he would turn to the DIRECTORY, and trace him out.
>
> Like a house, every paragraph in "ENQUIRE WITHIN" has its number,—and the INDEX is the DIRECTORY which will explain what Facts, Hints, and Instructions *inhabit* that number.
>
> For, if it be not a misnomer, we are prompted to say that "ENQUIRE WITHIN" is *peopled* with hundreds of ladies and gentlemen, who have approved of the plan of the work, and contributed something to its store of useful information. There they are, waiting to be questioned, and ready to reply. Within each page some one lives to answer for the correctness of the information imparted, just as certainly as where, in the window of a dwelling, you see a paper directing you to "ENQUIRE WITHIN", some one is there to answer you. HOUSEKEEPERS of experience live at Nos, 1, 30, 438, 1251 and 2091; old Dr. KITCHENER lives at 44; CAPTAIN CRAWLEY is to be found at 46 and 2568; ... and Dr. CLARK at 2384. In addition to these and many more, a DOCTOR lives at 475; a GARDENER at 249; a SCHOOLMASTER at 161 ...

This sample of the index entries shows their wholly engrossing nature.

Temper, Female, Management of
  Keep Your
Uncleanliness of Person, Depre-
  cated
Vulgarity, Avoidance of
W, Use of, for V, Enigma on
Water, Adulteration of
  as Beverage, Excellence of
  on the Brain, Remedy for
  Effect of, on Meat, if Left in,
  when Cooked
  Ecrustation of Certain Vessels
  by

Erect Position in
Hard, to Prepare for Washing
Hard, to Soften
Hot, Efficacy of
in Holland and England
Soft, to Prepare
Window-Curtains on Fire, How
  to Act
Work by Daylight Preferable in
  Winter
How to accomplish
Wow-Wow Sauce
Yorkshire, Dialect, Errors of
  Pudding

Another unusual feature of this index is its use to promote moral
precepts. Each of the book's 388 text pages has one, in small capi-
tals, as its headline, and the index is no exception to this stern rule.
So one is admonished as one searches; usually in rather glum fashion. The precept above the page of As is most appropriate to its
Place: AN INDEX IS A KEY TO A TREASURY. Splendid! (But
any index ... ?) Then, above B, we move to HONESTY IS A
STRONG STAFF TO LEAN UPON. Good thought, if not particularly apposite to information retrieval. And so through such
pious advice as STUDY NOT TO BEAUTIFY THY FACE,
BUT THY MIND; BUSYBODIES NEVER HAVE ANY-
THING TO DO; THE LANE OF BY-AND-BY LEADS TO
THE HOUSE OF NEVER.

Facing pages sometimes feature precepts that are related or that
continue across the double page. D-E casts double gloom with
FOR AGE AND WANT SAVE WHILE YOU MAY, opposite,
THERE ARE NONE POOR BUT SUCH AS GOD DIS-
OWNS. A comma at the end of the headline above P, KEEP ON
GOOD TERMS WITH YOUR WIFE, is the only indication that
this thought is continued above Q-R, YOUR STOMACH, AND
YOUR CONSCIENCE. Above Z, page 415, the editor sinks
thankfully back with ALL'S WELL THAT ENDS WELL.

Index of an opium-eater

The index to Thomas de Quincey's *Collected Writings* (edited by David Masson and published in 14 volumes by A. and C. Black in 1896-97) is proudly presented as 'compiled under the superintendence of Mr H. B. Wheatley, F. S. A., ... whose name ought to be a sufficient guarantee for the accuracy and thoroughness of this portion of the work'. 'Accuracy and thoroughness' seem not to exclude the vivid expression of vigorous opinion.

Aldermen not necessarily gluttons

Anecdotes, on eating peas with a knife

Aristocracy, feelings of the, with regard to letting their houses

Bed, early retirement to, of the Ancients

Bull, Irish, what is it?

Bulls, Milton's

Christenings, Royal, often hurried

Coffee, atrocious in England

Cookery, English, the rudest of barbarous devices

Devonshire men good-looking

Dogs in Greece, a nuisance

Fleas in Greece

Greece, Ancient, its people a nation of swindlers

Horses, weeping

Hotels, colossal, of America

Johnson, Dr, at dinner, an indecent spectacle

Leibnitz, died partly from the fear of not being murdered

Life, instances of long-sustained powers of, in a murdered woman

Lisbon earthquake and its effect on the religion of Germany

Mahomet not a great man

Meat, barbarous cookery of, in Great Britain

Muffins, eating, a cause of suicide

Music, English obtuseness to good

Newspapers, the fearfulness of their contents

Pig-grunting, mimicry of

Readers, actors usually bad

Rhinoceros, first sale of a

Servants, England the paradise of household

Solon, what did he do for Homer?

Spitting, art of

Talk, too much in the world

Toothache, that terrific curse

Translation really impossible

Veracity a marked feature in the English character

Waterton's adventure with a crocodile

Women, can die grandly

20th century

Vainglorious introduction

Percy Fitzgerald was an Irish writer, the author of more than two hundred volumes, a sculptor, and friend of Charles Dickens. He was also editor of the volume of *The Life of Samuel Johnson and The Journal of a Tour to the Hebrides*, both by James Boswell, published by Sands & Company of London in 1900, and himself provided the index.

The prefatory note, half a page long, preceding the 24-page, double-column 'Full index of names, topics and opinions' to the texts, shows a huge vaingloriousness, with sneers at fellow indexers – a most unbecoming display.

> This Index, which has been made by the Editor himself, after considerable thought and labour, will, it is hoped, be found clear of the common defects which attend most indexes. No proper or sufficient index can be made vicariously: it requires a thorough acquaintance with the book treated, so as to anticipate by a sort of instinct what topics the reader would desire to search for. Indexes are generally too minutely elaborate, too meagre, or too indefinite. The common meagre index, that fills three or four pages, leaves out everything that the reader wishes to look for, and is too general.

Let readers judge the justice of this self-praise from these sample entries. Punctuation is cited exactly as in the original.

Amusement, taste for, decays in age, Johnson on. 'The lad does not care for the child's rattle,' etc.

Are votes gained by speeches?

'Blockhead,' Johnson applies the term to a housemaid in Birmingham

Coarse language in the House of Commons preferable to veiled genteel attacks

'Completes what he has to say, Oglethorpe never'

Dogged veracity in a Duke of Devonshire

Earth and stone in Scotland: like a man in rags, its naked skin is always peeping out

'Filled up places are always of great depth,' Johnson's sarcastic remark at Col

Friend, one more active, in assisting friends by his labour never was than Johnson

Gratitude not found among gross people

---

*I for my part venerate the inventor of Indexes; and
I know not to whom to yield the preference, either to
Hippocrates, who was the first great anatomiser of
the human body, or to that unknown labourer in literature who first laid open the nerves and arteries
of a book.*

Isaac D'Israeli, *Literary Miscellanies* (1796)

Blanket pulping

Caliban's Guide to Letters, published in 1903, was an early product of Hilaire Belloc's prolific and varied career as an author. The book takes a satirical look at the world of writing and publishing – and through this at a number of other topics. The title used above is the one by which it is usually known, but the full title-page reads as follows: *The Aftermath or, Gleanings from a Busy Life, called upon the outer cover for purpose of sale Caliban's Guide to Letters*. This extended title nicely catches the light-hearted satirical note sustained throughout the book and into the index.

The most obvious feature of the index is that every entry is given the same page reference. The A section includes:

Abingdon, History of, by Lord Charles Gamber, see Pulping, p. 187
Action, Combination of, with Plot, Powerful Effect of in Modern Novels, see Pulping, p. 187
Affection, Immoderate, for our own Work, Cure of, see Pulping, p. 187
Amusements of Printers and Publishers, see Pulping, p. 187
Art, Literary, Ultimate End of, see Pulping, p. 187

and it ends with

W, X, Y, Z, See Pulping, p. 187.

Whether this final entry strikes a note of impatience or of despair, or simply denotes a shortage of further ideas, it has to be admitted that the joke palls well before the end of the index. The point that is being made in many of the entries (if, indeed, there ever was one) is now probably irretrievably lost, but some entries represent favourite Belloc targets still readily recognizable. For example, his continuing bitterness over the failure of All Souls, Oxford, to elect him to a fellowship is given vent in the entry:

All Souls, College of, see Pulping, p. 187

Some of those from whom he differed in the course of a life of controversy also feature; e.g.:

> Curzon, Lord, his Literary Works, ...
> India, Lord Curzon's views on, ...
> Milner, Lord, Proclamations of, ...

All these are consigned to the pulping machine, as are various aspects of the literary world. Among the literary jokes, we find:

> Authorship, Vanity of Human ...
> Boethius, Decline in Sale, of Works of, ...
> Daniel in Lion's Den Compared to a Just Author ...
> Dowagers, Novels written by, ...
> Genius, Indestructibility of, ...

and there are jibes at the ways of publishers which may be either good-humoured or barbed:

> Advertisement, Folly and Waste of, ...
> Cabs, Necessity of, to Modern Publisher, ...
> Cabs to Authors, Unwarrantable Luxury, ...
> Curse, Publishers a, ...

There is, it would seem, in this index almost the material for a psychoanalytical study of Belloc and his *idées fixes*.

Caliban's Guide was republished in 1920 in a composite volume which also included another of Belloc's literary skits, *Lambkin's Remains*. For this new edition the text was reset and repaginated, with the result that the section entitled 'On Remainders and Pulping', originally on pp. 187-9, is now to be found on pp. 156-9, but the index was printed exactly as in the first edition. Was the reiteration of a now meaningless reference to 'Pulping' on p. 187 a deliberate extension of the joke or – as seems more likely – an oversight on the part of the publisher's editorial staff and (if he saw the new edition in proof) of the author? We shall probably never know, unless there is a bibliographical and literary enquiry bureau in heaven.

J.A.V.

Mythical indexing

Sir James Frazer's history of myth and religion, *The Golden Bough*, was first published in two volumes in 1890; then in three volumes in 1900 and in twelve, 1911-15. The 756-page single volume abridged by Frazer himself was published in 1922 by Macmillan & Co. (reissued by Chancellor Press, 1994). These sample entries from its 42-page index make one long to read the text.

Africa, magicians, especially rain-makers, as chiefs and kings in; human gods in; rules of life or taboos observed by kings in; reluctance of people to tell their own names in; seclusion of girls at puberty in; dread and seclusion of menstruous women in; birth-trees in
__, North, charms to render bridegroom impotent in
__, South, disposal of cut hair and nails in; magic use of spittle in; story of the external soul in
__, West, magical functions of chiefs in; reverence for silk-cotton trees in; kings forced to accept office in; fetish kings in; traps set for souls in; custom as to blood shed on the ground; propitiation of dead leopard in
Animals, homoeopathic magic of; association of ideas common to the; rain-making by means of; injured through their shadows; propitiation of the spirits of the slain; torn to pieces and devoured in religious rites; ... belief in the descent of men from; ... perhaps deemed embodiments of witches
Anointing stones, in order to avert

bullets from absent warriors; in a rain-charm
Apple-tree, barren women roll under, to obtain offspring; straw man placed on oldest; torches thrown at; as life-index of boys
Bag, souls of persons deposited in a
Beating a man's garments instead of the man; frogs, as a rain-charm
Bed-clothes, contagious magic of bodily impressions on
Birds, cause headache through clipped hair; absent warriors called
Cat's cradle, forbidden to boys among the Esquimaux
Cattle, magical stones for increase of; influence of tree-spirits on; crowned; Yule Boar given to the; lighted brands carried round
Charms, to prevent the sun from going down
Chastity observed for sake of absent persons; as a virtue not understood by savages
Clothes, magic sympathy between a person and his
Columbia, British, use of magic

instruments to procure fish in; taboos imposed on parents of twins in; belief regarding a physician and his patient's soul; rites of initiation in

Conception in women caused by trees

Continence, required during search for sacred cactus; enjoined on people during rounds of sacred pontiff; by hunters and fishers; by workers in salt-pans

Departmental kings of nature

Dogs crowned

East Indies, pregnant women forbidden to tie knots; reluctance of people to tell their own names; bringing back the Soul of the Rice; the Rice-mother in the

Fairies, averse to iron

Feet of enemies eaten

Fish, magical image to procure; sacred; treated with respect by fishing tribes; external soul in a golden

Foreskins used in rainmaking

Gorillas, lives of persons bound up with those of

Gout, transferred to trees

Holiness, and pollution not differentiated by savages; conceived

as a dangerous virus; as a dangerous physical substance which needs to be insulated

Hooks used in magic; to catch souls

Hyaenas, supposed power over men's shadow

Impregnation of women by the sun

Jar, the evil of a whole year shut up in

Jars, wind kept by priests in

Lemon, external souls of ogres in

Magnets thought to keep brothers at unity

Parrots' eggs, a signal of death

Pear-tree as protector of cattle; as life-index of a girl

Sardines worshipped by Indians of Peru

Standing on one foot, custom of

Tobacco, used as an emetic

Tobacco smoke, priest inspired by

Toothache, transferred to enemies

Twins, taboos laid on parents of; supposed to possess magical powers; associated with salmon, and the grizzly bear; called children of the sky; water poured on graves of; parents of, thought to be able to fertilise plantain tree

Whale's ghost, fear of injuring

You are old, Father William ...

A. Lapthorn Smith's expressed intention in his *How to be Useful and Happy from Sixty to Ninety* (John Lane, 1922) is to overcome the erroneous idea that because a man has reached the age of 60 he must give up all his interests in life and spend the rest of his days in idleness and sorrow. This worthy intention informs every entry of the index, a fascinating blend of serious indexing, deliberate humour, and some remarkable examples of accidental humour deriving from his very shaky technique – he breaks several rules of indexing – in the course of producing an index that is a delight to read or to dip into.

> Absurdity of voluntary retirement at sixty
> Adding ten years to life
> Alcohol as cure for insomnia, very bad
> All day in garden
> Beard, long white, don't wear
> Carriage and pair shortens life
> Cause of insomnia must be found
> Cook, good, source of danger to elderly men
> Crime to die rich
> Engine drivers over sixty, what to do with them
> Garrett, Mrs., of Penge, active voter at 102
> If no relatives, spend on poor
> Young people, company of, at sixty, how to keep

G.N.K.

Holiday exuberance

Together by Norman Douglas (published by Chapman and Hall in 1923) is a lively and evocative account of a sojourn in various Austrian mountain villages. The six-page index is partly a list of proper names, partly a somewhat casual collection of finger posts for prospective ramblers in Alpine foothills; but above all it is a bit of fun, obviously designed to comfort the reader who regrets having come to the end of the text. The index is as informative, colourful and exuberant as the book itself. Here are some typical entries:

Anna, old nurse, passion for idiots and corpses, 105; gets it hot, 49; shakes chocolate from a tree, 104

Brunnemacher, father, mountaineer, presumably hirsute, 17; son, indubitably hirsute, 18

Cocoa, an abomination, 10

Gluttony, when to be discouraged, 12; when permissible, 13

Grandfather, paternal, a feudal monster, always spick-and-span, 196; excavates in imagination the Akropolis at Athens, 99; tells Prince Consort how to manage Queen Victoria, 100; sometimes mistaken for an angel, 199; vicious to the last, 201

Grandmother, insists upon recitations from Marmion, 54 ; gets them, 55

Hare, how to shoot, 123; how not to cook, 203

Peasants, their grievances, 57; catch pneumonia supervising cows at pasture, 104

Slippins, dog, specializes in fleas and beer, 98

Theocritus, seldom caught napping, 96

Tiefis village, 22, 96; visit to its tavern, 26; another visit, 65; another, 95 another, 118; destroyed by fire, 166

Townbred persons, often incomplete, 45-7

Weisskreuz Hotel, its manager well worth making love to, 103

Norman Knight referred in *The Indexer* in 1970 to 'those deliberately amusing indexes for which Norman Douglas is famous', quoting from the index to Douglas's *Limerick Book* (published by Anthony Blond) the sole entry:

Twickenham, unreasonable complaint by female resident of

G.N.K.

The index belligerent

Douglas Haig, 1st Earl Haig, was one of the most controversial British commanders of the First World War, and has been persistently condemned for his 'attack at all costs' mentality. David Lloyd George, minister of munitions, war secretary and subsequently coalition prime minister during that war, was known for his distrust of the military at all levels. In the index to his *War Memoirs* (Odham's Press, 1938), the entry for Haig gives full vent to Lloyd George's hostility, in eight packed columns of tiny type, containing such charges as:

> failure of his strategy at the Somme
> misleads Cabinet about Italian front
> prefers to gamble with men's lives than to admit error
> his fanciful estimates of manpower
> neglects defences of Fifth Army
> his conspiracy to destroy General Reserve
> his attempt to shirk blame for March 1918 defeat
> misstatements about Italian reinforcements

I.D.C.

Shavian provocativeness

George Bernard Shaw's prefaces to his own plays, 'forming a series of pamphlets and essays on current political and social problems, are quite journalistic in character, and cover a period of nearly thirty years', as he describes them in the Introduction to *Prefaces,* the collection published by Constable and Company in 1934, when Shaw was, as he tells us, 'a sage of seventy-eight'. The text makes 777 pages; the index 24, double-column. The indexer is not credited, but the hand of the author himself seems evident throughout, in the deliberately provocative style and assertions, and reinforcement there, at gleefully disproportionate length, of the lessons of the text.

The choice as to expatiation is considered. There are several undifferentiated strings of page references – 17 for flogging, 19 for liberty, 15 for Nietzsche, 31 for Ibsen before his subheads start; but a single reference may be expanded where the author wishes to repeat his point. There is certainly no attempt to keep subheadings concise, and Shaw joyously seized the opportunity to restate his views – to such effect that the entries for children and doctors each take one column of the index, that for marriage takes one and a half, and his own entry – such a full and detailed biographical summary that one can hardly feel the need to consult the text cited – exceeds two columns.

We print below a selection of the most entertaining entries.

Doctors, a surgeon has a pecuniary interest in operations – the more he mutilates, the higher his fee; agree to agree on the point that the doctor is always right; ... bring comfort and reassurance to the relatives, and sometimes death to the patient; ... operations are recorded successful if the patient leaves alive; ... statistics should be kept of all illnesses of doctors and their families; ... they themselves die of the very diseases they profess to cure

Jesus Christ, a highly-civilized, cultivated person; adapted himself to the fashionable life of his time; ... was a communist ...

Love ... an appetite which is destroyed for the moment by its gratification; ... cases of chronic lifelong love ought to be sent to the doctor; entire preoccupation with, is a nuisance; ... is a tyranny requiring special safeguards; ... proposals made under its influence should not be binding

Morals, are like teeth: the more decayed they are the more it hurts to touch them

Shaw, George Bernard ...
boyhood and education – ... : early employments, and as a young man; he took care to dodge every commercial opening, and became an incorrigible unemployable; at about the age of thirteen seeks employment with a firm of cloth merchants; spent four and a half years as a clerk and cashier in Dublin; employed by the Way Leave Department of the Edison Telephone Company; assists in counting the votes at Leyton election; a shy youth and ignorant of social routine, although some may have found him insufferable, aggressive, and impudent; contradicted everyone from whom he thought he could learn anything; his diabolical opinions as a young man; his moustaches, eyebrows, and sarcastic nostrils; says 'I had never thought I was to be a great man simply because I had always taken it as a matter of course'; ... emerges from obscurity and is applauded as the most humorously extravagant paradoxer in London: miscellaneous – a natural-born mountebank, he first caught the ear of the British public on a cart in Hyde Park; acquires a superhuman insensitiveness to praise or blame, which leads to indifference to the publication or performance of his works; advertises himself; as a pianist, denies that he is original; difference between the spirit of Tolstoy and the spirit of Mr. Shaw; found it impossible to believe anything until he could conceive it as a scientific hypothesis; ... people meeting him in private were surprised at his mildness and sociability; says 'Whether it be that I was born mad or a little too sane, my kingdom was not of this world: I was at home only in the realm of my imagination'; The Complete Outsider; the least ambitious of men ... has risen by sheer gravitation, too industrious by acquired habit to stop working; ...

Women ... entirely preoccupied with affection are nuisances; ... home life makes them unfit for human society

What indexes! Independent indexing principles

G. Norman Knight wrote of A. P. Herbert as 'the supreme artist in the field of humorous indexing ... wittiest of writers, he is not afraid of letting his wit penetrate his indexes. ... The humour springs largely from overstatement and understatement, from alluring, mischievous or satirical descriptions and from the choice of unexpected and unlikely key words and altogether disarming cross-references. ... to read them through is sheer joy. Indeed they seem designed rather for entertainment than as reference tools. On the other hand, coming across some particularly alarming or outrageous statement in a heading or subheading sends the reader flying at once to the appropriate page to find out what it is all about.'

Knight writes of Herbert's index to his treatise on the English language, *What a Word* (1935), 'To be properly savoured, the 40-page index must be literally read through, not merely referred to.' It includes these assessments:

ABLATIVE: Shameless indifference to the, of Business Man

ADVERTISERS: No right to injure English language with barbarous inventions or wanton errors,

ALL of Us, So Say: Believed not, strictly, correct

BANKRUPTCIES: Attributed to time and treasure squandered in verbose business correspondence (and see Offices)

DRIVE: Fanciful use of, as in 'lack of drive' denoting anaemic policy of H.M. Government learnedly discussed

ENGLISH Language: Strange neglect of, by bodies and Societies eager to interfere in every other human activity

JOURNALIST: Capacity for continual amazement, considered

Impossibility of surprising, in private life, noted

Injuries to English language by, viewed in just proportion

PLAIN ENGLISH: Queer delusion of British Man that he talks

ZEE: The American barbarous use of

Believed inferior to British 'Zed'

Herbert's account of his lively career as a Burgess of Oxford University from 1935 to 1948, *Independent Member*, published in 1952, includes these eccentric entries in its index:

AIR, the disappointing

ALL SOULS, Christian behaviour; rash betting at

ASTOR, LADY, declines to buy author a drink

ATTLEE, RT, HON. CLEMENT, ... doodles; sensible; not

AWFUL WARNINGS, to Young Man, in House of Commons [12 page references]

BIG BEN, lying by, deplored

BLOCK, my, is not knocked off

BOARD OF TRADE, President of, takes his feet off the table

BOAT BUILDER, un-Christian remark by a divine

'BUFFOON', unfeeling use of

CANNIBALISM, as aid to advancement

CHESTERTON, G. K., on Faith; (sorry again)

DONS, more decorative than you would think

'*Gambler's Despair*', believed only greyhound mentioned by name in Parliament

HORSE, I kill a; entertainment tax on; and Neptune

'IUNAITED STAITS', start to world language

'JUST WHERE YOU ARE', disturbing episode

KRUGER, PRESIDENT, a flat-earther

LOOTING, I escape a charge of

MIXED METAPHOR, a beauty

NOEL-BAKER, RT. HON. PHILIP: I am nice to; is not nice to me

PADDOCK OF INGENIOUS MONSTERS

'USUAL CHANNELS', not always bubbling with joy about Independents

Further index goodies from A.P. Herbert are found in his volume, *The Thames* (1966), such as:

SUICIDE: respectful treatment of females attempting [The allusion is to the River Police Station, at Waterloo, the only one afloat in the world. Here there is a hot bath and when a woman is dragged out of the water she is placed in the bath *in her clothes.*]

TAP, THE: avoided abroad by Londoners fearlessly approached at home

— and in *Sundials – Old and New* (1967), thus:

EARTH, MOTIONS OF: bold attempt to explain, by author

ECLIPTIC, THE,: defined; deplored

JEANS, SIR JAMES: not co-operative

MIRACLE: author does Isaiah's

NOVELTIES SHYLY CLAIMED BY AUTHOR [13 are listed]

SEXTANT: gift of, causes this book, and much trouble besides

G.N.K.

: 30 :

A discordant index

Essays in Musical Analysis by Donald Tovey was published in six serious-seeming volumes from the Oxford University Press, 1935-39. The final volume includes supplementary essays on several composers, glossary, and index.

Assuming the (uncredited) index to be the work of the author, it would seem that, exhausted by his labours, he took the task of indexing as an opportunity for relaxation and merrymaking in print. Consider the following selection of its entries, quoted verbatim and as punctuated:

Ablative Absolute, *see* Passacaglia.
Agelastic Philosophy, untenability of, *see* Edwards.
Agnostic, *see* Dachshund.
Appendicitis, *see* Cadenza. [There is no entry for Cadenza.]
Beaver as lace-maker, *see* Continuo.
Bernard, St., *see* Pope.
'Bo!', Haydn's Lion says, v. 139.
Brahms, [no forename. 12 lines of undifferentiated page numbers followed by nearly a column of subheadings with page numbers, but no reference to hedgehogs]
Bruckner, [11 lines with no reference to agnosticism, dachshunds or the Pope]
Continuo, i. 155-6, v. 34, vi. 157.
Critics, *see* Experts.
Dachshund, *see* Bernard.
Edwards, i. 149 *et passim.*
Elephant, *see* Haydn.
Experts, *see* Critics.

Grocer, *see* Hindemith.
Haydn, Joseph, [an entry more than a column long. Three inches down comes 'not an elephant', v. 137]
Hedgehog, *see* Brahms.
Hindemith, Paul, iv. 172-6, vi. 148, 150, 163; and sugar, iv. 174
Loch Ness, *see* Wagner and the Paris Opera.
Monster, *see* Loch Ness.
Passacaglia, i. 115.
Pope, *see* Bruckner.
Sand, *see* Sugar.
Sugar, *see* Grocer.
Wagner, Richard, [9 lines of page numbers; more than half a column of subheadings with page numbers, no reference to the Paris Opera]
Wagner, Siegfried, iv. 128-9.
Wagnerian Leit-motiv, i. 39, ii. 81, iii. 153, 203, iv. 54, 70; and the Paris Opera, vi. 112.

Indexmanship

Stephen Potter achieved great success, even a devoted cult, with his sequence of humorous works beginning with *Gamesmanship* (Rupert Hart-Davis, 1947) in which he devised and delineated 'the art of winning games without actually cheating'. He thus gave a new word and concept to the English language, defined in *Collins English Dictionary* as: '**one-upmanship** n. Informal. the art or practice of achieving or maintaining an advantage over others'.

The 'Glossarial index' to *Gamesmanship* itself gives some demonstration of the techniques of putting your opponent ill at ease, discomfitted. The reader must surely feel a bewilderment attributable only to ignorance on his part – thus, a discomposed inferiority. Note also the patronising assumption of the necessity for otiose explanation.

The parentheses all appear *sic* in the original.

Billiards, use of telephone in; when to give advice in; use of Improved Primitive in

Bowls, use of luncheon-interval in

Odoreida, G., perhaps Gamesmanship's most brilliant product. Origin unknown, youth unknown, obscure middle period. Influence of mother on (deleted from this edition); infantile experience of (ditto); lawn tennis racket especially constructed by; his match with Bzo

Polo, natural history asides in

Quotation marks, in Gamesmanship, the scoring of points, e.g., while in play, by the use of inept, trite, distracting or rude quotations or misquotations (*quote* vb2., Du: *quoots*, Goth: *vas.*)

Rushington's drivel

Simpson, R.; drinksmanship and; origin of Simpson's statue

Squash-rackets; nose-blowing and; leaking roof, used in; and Ruggership

Sussexmanship, or the use and abuse of scenic beauty. (*Sussex*, name of Sussex, the county)

Tipmanship

Winner's heartiness

Tale-telling

An index itself can tell a pretty tale. This narrative entry from F.A. Pottle's index of 1950 to Boswell's *London Journal* (Edinburgh University Press) surely tells you all you could wish to know of this affair. It is an example of the unwisdom of consulting the index before reading the text, if one wishes to retain any element of suspense.

> Lewis, Mrs (Louisa), actress. JB to call Louisa in journal; receives JB; JB visits; JB's increased feeling for; JB discusses love with; JB anticipates delight with; JB lends two guineas to; disregards opinion of world; discusses religion with JB; JB entreats to be kind; uneasiness of discourages JB; JB declares passion for; promises to make JB blessed; ... makes assignation with JB; consummation with JB interrupted; ... JB likes better and better; JB's felicity delayed; ... JB afraid of a rival; JB feels coolness for; ... JB incredulous at infection from; JB enraged at perfidy of; ... JB asks his two guineas back; ...

I certainly think that the best book in the world would owe the most to a good index, and the worst book, if it had but a single, good thought in it, might be kept alive by it.

Horace Binney, *Letter to S. A. Allibone* (1868)

: 33 :
With tongue in (both) cheeks

G. V. Carey produced in 1951 an excellent little guide to indexing, *Making an Index*, published by the Cambridge University Press, 13 pages long. A review in the *Times Literary Supplement* suggested that the work might have been better for an index of its own. In the second edition, published in the same year, Carey observed:

> An index to a work of about a dozen pages can hardly hope even in full dress to be within the bounds of decency. Yet the reviewer, though he may have had his tongue in his cheek, has put the author on his mettle and tempted him to take up the challenge.
>
> In case there should be any reader so guileless as to be led astray, it had been the author's intention to give some distinguishing mark to all those entries in the index that he had devised with *his* tongue in his cheek – occasionally even (as it were) in both cheeks. As the work proceeded, however, he became so deeply involved in *Paddenda* (let alone his determination to include every letter of the alphabet) that the opposite course seemed to be called for.

These are some of the entries for this index that appeared *without* an asterisk affirming their necessary or helpful nature.

Anybody, mere page-numbers not of the slightest use to, 7

Chase, wild goose. *See* Von Kluck

Cherry, twice bitten, once shy. *See* Cross-references

Common sense, use your, 9, 15, and *pass*.

Eye in, getting your, 5

Goose chase, wild. *See* Kluck, von

Haystack, looking for needle in, 4

Horrid word. *See* Alphabetisation

Kluck, von. *See* Von Kluck

Omniscient, indexers not always, 4

Order, alphabetical. *See* Horrid word

Perfection, counsel of, 3

Sense, common. *See* Common sense

Spoon-feeding, 12

Temptations, indexers', 3, 12

Von Kluck. *See* Kluck, von

What not to do. *See* Anybody, Earl of Beaconsfield, von Kluck, etc., etc.

Wild goose chase. *See* Kluck, von

X. *See* Index, Prefixes

York, New, missing, 10

Yourself in the users' place, put, 6-7, 12

Zealand, New, 10

: 34 :
Droit de fille

The daughter of Waldo E. Nelson, editor of the 7th edition of *Textbook of Pediatrics* (W. B. Saunders, Philadelphia, 1959), compiled its index and, in jocular vein, inserted an entry conveying her opinion of her father's work:

> Birds, for the, 1-1413

The line was missed, and allowed to remain in subsequent editions.

: 35 :
Let me help

The index to *The English Village Community and the Enclosure Movements* by W. E. Tate (Gollancz, 1967) shows a most engaging anxiety to be helpful. All these 'asides' appear *sic*.

> Bacon, Sir Francis (not 'Lord' B.)
> Coke, Sir Edward (not 'Lord Coke')
> Cooke, John (not of course the regicide but a contemporary)
> Young, Arthur, fl. 1808, not the famous Arthur (above),
>   but a contemporary of the same name [no page number given]

: 36 :
Sequential subheadings

From Desmond Ryan's *The Fenian Chief: A Biography of James Stephens* (published in Dublin by Gill & Son, 1967):

O'Brien, An:
    never turns his back on an enemy, 32
    would never retreat from fields in which ancestors were kings, 33
    does, 34

: 37 :
The hit direct

Bernard Levin's own index to his contemporary history, *The Pendulum Years: Britain and the Sixties* (Jonathan Cape, 1970), gives full rein to his vigorous opinions.

Brooke, Henry; removed from House of Commons (qv); plans to deport girl for £2 theft; refuses asylum to Robert Soblen (qv); returns Soblen's corpse to United States; conviction that there should be no place in House of Commons for

Griffith-Jones, Mervyn: prosecutes *Lady Chatterley's Lover* (qv) *passim*; calls no evidence against Penguin Books (qv); 'wife or servants'; 'womb and bowels'; and marriage; mind 'unable to see beauty where it exists'; sincerity; ... and 'night of sensual passion', and ruin of and corruption of the country; does not shoot himself; prosecutes Fanny Hill (qv); horrified; calls no evidence once again; and author's intent; face missing

Hailsham, Lord (frequently Quintin Hogg): chief Pharisee; denounces John Profumo (qv); sober; defies Whips; eccentric view of Whipping; rebuked by Lord Balfour of Inchrye (qv); rebuked by Reginald Paget, M.P. *(qv)*; rebuked by George Wigg *(qv)*; shape of; and involuntary ennoblement; and renunciation of peerage; and Tory succession; and *Lady Chatterley's Lover (qv)*

legal profession, naivety of

'Wife or servants', see Griffith-Jones, Mervyn

: 38:

Indigestible index

Man and Food, by Magnus Pyke, was published in 1970 in Weidenfeld & Nicolson's World University Library series, and deals with nutritional knowledge and current research. It has 247 text pages, heavily illustrated. Information retrieval problems start there; the page numbers are in upper, outer page corners, and usually do not occur where there is any illustration or table, as most of these are set at the tops of the pages – often with the caption at the top of the page opposite. Left-side chapter openings also have no page numbers. Many pages thus are unnumbered; but the index references to lead to them are so poor that their lack hardly seems crucial, after all.

The index is set triple-column over three pages, with numerals in bold referring to illustrations. All its page references are single, double (24-5, 24-25, 60-1, 60-61, *sic*, all occur) or single followed by *et seq.* Closer discrimination is apparently not possible, even where the index entry copies the chapter or section heading. Thus, chapter 10, 'The evolution of technological processes', pages 168-85, is indexed as 'TECHNOLOGICAL PROCESSES, evolution of', 168 *et seq.*, while chapter 7, 'Deficiency diseases', pages 110-27, manages only DEFICIENCY 110 and DISEASE 110.

Three pages of index to 243 of text seems skimpy – nevertheless, there are many duplicated entries, including the eleven lines under FOOD PRESERVATION, which are repeated in full under PRESERVATION OF FOOD, with a line there added (BY IRRADIATION 201, 202-3). Space saved by substituting cross-references might have been allotted to glosses for such bare, unexplained entries as:

> Bonteheuwel; Braconnot; Clary; Ernmer; Ergosterol; Ghee; Gracilis; Hemeralopia; Phytopthora; Terpenes; Voit

(Respectively, these are a settlement near Cape Town; a French chemist; a spice; hulled wheats; a chemical compound; clarified butter; a muscle; night-blindness; a fungus; oil constituents; a German chemist.)

Strangest, though, is the placing of entries. Some subjects can be found only as obscure subheadings, not having their own entry. CATTLE, COWS, CHILDREN and COOKING (perhaps the indexer was allergic to the letter C?) can be found only under:

Breeds of cattle 32, 51 [actually pages 32-3 deal with the live-weight of
    cattle that land in Africa can sustain; no reference to Africa either]
Endocrine glands of cow 45 [this is the only mention in the index of
    cows, whose blood plasma is tabulated on page 43, udder described
    on 44, emotions on pages 45-6, and appetites 46-50, with photo-
    graphs of two on page 51]
Food/cooking of 10-11
Weight of school children 230

Terminology is quite unsettled and disordered. ANIMALS has three subheadings, but no reference to WILD ANIMALS, which is a separate entry under W, nor to cattle or cows, so slighted here. FOOD yields the following mixture of main and subheadings:

Food
    colour in 184 [duplicated under colouring as 184: a full-page table]
    cooking of 10-11
    texture of 205, 205, 206 [not entered under T]
Food preservation [11 lines, duplicated under P]
Food synthesis 208 et seq. 210 [sic]
    cost of 223
Food technology 168 et seq.
    effects of in Africa 169 [still no reference to Africa under A]

Compare and contrast with these the following:

Synthesis [an eight-line entry, not including COST]
Synthetic food 208 et seq. 210
    nutritional value of 222
Technological processes, evolution of 168 et seq.
Technology, effect of 246

The Frank Muir index

When Douglas Matthews compiled the index to *The Frank Muir Book: An Irreverent Companion to Social History* (Heinemann, 1976), the book's author/editor, comedian Frank Muir, told him to make it as jokey as he wished. But the indexer felt there was enough humour already in the text, and that he couldn't compete with that – or, indeed, that he might even kill the joke in the text by trying.

There was one exception. Matthews explains, 'In the General Index under "audiences" is a subheading, "roast Lamb". This is a reference to the audience reaction to the opening night of Lamb's farce, *Mr. H*, which was hissed and booed.'

Here are some of the riper plums in this index that need no gilding and make the user long to turn to the item indicated.

Bible: Isaiah, on beans; silent
  on theatre
bluebottle flies, declared
  unpalatable
cauliflowers, pretentiousness of
chorus girls, knees knocked
Douglas, Norman, on infidelity
  with publishers
Hepburn, Katherine, emotional
  range described
Landor, Walter Savage, spoils
  violets with cook
length (human), and distaste
moles, unpalatability

nuns, forbidden beans
organs (musical instruments),
  in Russia; of hogs
pancakes, and decay of learning
teeth, cleaning with wine; cleaning with knife
toothache, unhelpful music for
trousers, added to Sistine Chapel
  nudes; and lanky tastelessness
turbot, and value of reading;
  presentation
ugliness, rivalry over
underwear, in ballet

Prejudicial introduction

Hans Wellisch (in *Indexing from A to Z*, H. W. Wilson 1995, page 284) called the index to Peter Schickele's *The Definitive Biography of P.D.Q. Bach* (1976) 'a brilliant spoof on indexes'. The index is preceded by this highly judgemental introductory note:

> Important references are given in boldface. Italicized numbers indicate fleeting references, whereas numbers in parentheses refer to mere implications or unwarranted extrapolations. Asterisks are used to identify particularly distasteful passages.

The index has no boldface locators. A typical entry is:

> Bach, J. S., vii, (ix), (xiii), 3*, 4-5, 6, 11, 15-18 ... (and so on and on for a total of some 30 locators).

But perhaps Schickele has a point here, Wellisch asks?

Forbearance

Great Operatic Disasters by Hugh Vickers (Macmillan, 1979) includes the forbearing entry, with no page references given::

> Incompetence – better not specified

Literally food for thought?

The degree of literalism shown in the index to *Equality* by Keith Joseph and Jonathan Sumption (Murray, 1979) can hardly be swallowed. Under the uncalled-for entry 'Menus' appear, *sic:*

> Menus:
> apples, 83
> bread, 49
> cakes, 12, 50, 84-88, 105-106, 112
> carrots, 24
> manna, 86
> omelettes, 44
> salt, 112

The book treats of economics and politics. These entries refer respectively to: on page 83, the principle of distribution, as for instance of a thousand apples among a hundred people; page 49, whether lack of bread implies lack of freedom; page 12, 'a cake-sharing mentality'; 50, fixed and divisible cakes; 84-88, 'Cakes: their use and abuse' (i.e. sharing out of); 105-106, 'What goes into the cake?'; 112, 'the value of the national cake'; 24, the income tax rating analogy of 'donkeys in children's cartoons trotting forever onwards towards the carrot suspended from a stick attached to their neck'; 86, the fruits of the productive process 'likened to the distribution of heavenly manna'; 44, Beatrice Webb quoted as remarking of trucks of political prisoners, 'you can't make an omelette without breaking eggs'; – and, on page 112, 'Some egalitarians have now begun to concede that figures compiled on that basis should be taken with a pinch of ...'

Yes.

Egoism rampant

A Man of Honour by Joseph Bonanno (Deutsch, 1983) is the self-aggrandizing autobiography of a Sicilian Mafia leader or 'Godfather'. Its ten-page index (to 406-page text) shares this tendency regarding the book's main character. Bonanno's entry takes nearly a full page, including the subheads:

> generosity of; handsomeness of; intellect of; language skills of; tact of; wit of

Following some of these encomia to the only text indicated – sometimes just half a sentence – we find that:

> 'handsomeness of, 175' leads only to, 'In general, people considered me an attractive man';
> 'intellect of, 176', to 'They kindly praised my charm and intelligence';
> 'wit of, 168', to 'They used to say that I was the toasting champion of the dinner table' (no example is vouchsafed)

The technique is used against others, though, either as disguise or heavy sarcasm. Under 'Luciano, Charlie' is included a somewhat startling subhead, in gangland context;

> literary sophistication of, 14, 161

and under 'Magaddino, Stefano', also is listed,

> 'literary sophistication of, 14'.

Turning to these references, we find that page 161 refers to Charlie Luciano thus: 'Although illiterate, he possessed a shrewd intelligence and level-mindedness that made him a good leader and superb organizer'.

So this is literary sophistication . . . ? And in the Introduction, which begins on page 11, we find:

> Men such as Charlie Luciano, . . . and Stefano Magaddino were baffled whenever I would slip a literary allusion into our conversations. When I spoke Italian, they often complained that I used words they did not understand. They had grown up in the impoverished fields of Sicily or in the tenement streets of America. Their language was coarse and expedient.

: 44 :

Kiss and have it told

The enticing tales of Samuel Pepys's amours are boldly recounted in the index to R.C. Latham's 1983 index to his 11-volume edition of the diary. This was awarded the Wheatley Medal for an outstanding index, and is described by Wellisch (*Indexing from A to Z*, page 320) as 'an outstanding example of a modern narrative index that manages to provide the necessary context for every indexed item with a minimum of verbiage'. These are typical, thoroughly entertaining examples:

> BAGWELL — wife of William: her good looks; P plans to seduce; visits; finds her virtuous and modest; asks P for place for her husband; P kisses; she grows affectionate; he caresses; she visits him; her resistance collapses in alehouse; amorous encounters with: at her house ...
>
> WILLET, Deb, companion to EP:
> APPEARANCE: good looks; grave and genteel
> AS EPS'S COMPANION : engaged; combs P's hair; ... EP angry with ...
> P'S AFFAIR WITH : P pleased with; EP jealous; P kisses; caresses; discovered by EP; her rage and P's guilt; P fears she must leave; prevented from seeing; her confession; and dismissal; P searches for; EP threatens to slit her nose; P never to see again; ... sees in street; EP makes jealous scenes; threatens him with hot tongs; he meets by chance; ... winks at P in street; moves to Greenwich ...
> SOCIAL : ... dances; plays cards; ...

It didn't work out that way ...

The index to *The Experts Speak* by Christopher Cerf and Victor Navasky (Pantheon Books, 1984) was described by Hans Wellisch (*Indexing from A to Z*, page 321) as 'hilarious ... a spoof of narrative indexing', and the book as 'a collection of cocksure statements concerning the future made by well-known authorities on diverse subjects who were sadly mistaken in their self-assumed role of prophets'. The indexer, Sidney Wolfe Cohen, decided that the index should mirror the book's tongue-in-cheek character; be highly detailed and accurate, and also parody 'indexes' and be funny enough to read for its own sake. Succeeding in all these aims, the index won the H. W. Wilson Company Award for Excellence in Indexing in 1984. Here are some typical entries.

alarm, no cause for:
  in eruption of Mount Pele
  in stock market crash
  on Titanic
atomic bombs, Creator's foolproof plans for preventing development of
automobiles, foreign: U.S. not to worry about; horse not to be replaced by
computers, home, no reason seen for

germs, as fictitious; heat generated by kisses as destructive of
Pickering, William Henry: on fallacy of expecting airplanes to reach speed of trains and cars; on uselessness of airplanes in war; on visionary notion of transatlantic passenger flights

H.H.W.

: 46 :

Monstrous entry

Computer-use was surely responsible for the entry, 'mammoth', in Macmillan's *Guide to Britain's Nature Reserves* (1984). The animal does not appear in the reserves; but the text includes a sentence beginning, 'This guide is a mammoth work ...'.

: 47 :

Conductor's contempt

Author-publisher Hunter Davies, a staunch resident of Carlisle, inserted in the otherwise blameless index of the second edition of his *The Good Guide to the Lakes* (Forster Davies, 1986), the mischievous cross-reference leading to Carlisle's rival town, in the layout . reproduced here:

The entry caused upset in Barrow, and the Town Clerk officially complained. The offending entry was removed from subsequent editions.

The terminology of the shrew

Dale Spender, a feminist who challenged conventional perceptions of the way we use words in *Man Made Language,* turned her attention to man-made indexes when she undertook the indexing of her own *Women of Ideas.* In *Scribbling Sisters* (published by Camden Press, 1986), a compilation of letters she exchanged with her sister, Lynne, during 1984, she wrote of the pleasures and frustrations of selecting or devising feminist index headings.

She made entries for 'loving husbands' and 'Radical men', listing Bertrand Russell and John Stuart Mill as examples, cross-referenced to 'champions of women's rights'. 'Completion complex' was to indicate 'the incompleteness of a woman without a man', ridiculing the concept. 'Disagreeable women' comprised many of the author's favourites. For 'Harassment' she expected a reference on every page. 'Economies' was followed by 'Female, (sexual economics)' with subheadings, 'Failure to get a man, lucky to get a man, trading one's person (marriage and prostitution)'. Spender claimed, 'it is a practical way of saying that we don't have to accept the classification system that men have devised'. She refrained from indexing men mentioned in the text, 'on the grounds that what is good for the gander is good for the goose ... how many indexes in books written by men make women invisible?'

Discovering some mistakes in the book, Spender added another entry, 'mistakes, author's'. Lynne Spender replied, 'Your index for *Women of Ideas* sounds marvellous ... I see it as a conscious effort to reconceptualise "Knowledge".'

: 49 :

Cramming it on to a page

Patrick Barlow's *All the World's a Globe, or from Lemur to Cosmonaut: Desmond Olivier Dingle's Concise History of the Human Race*, published by Methuen in 1987, is a splendid parody of a scholarly volume, with all its pseudo-appurtenances. Its final flourish is a (deliberately) cramped single-page index (by the author, an English actor and writer) including these entries:

Australia:
    Paradise on Earth 18
    author's deep interest in visiting 18
    see also New Zealand [there is no entry for New Zealand]
Australians, most delightful people of author's acquaintance 18
    (along with New Zealanders. Also Canadians. And Glaswegians, obviously)
Bronowski, Sir Jacob:
    greatest man who ever lived 115
Canada:
    author's deep affinity towards 109n
    availablity with regard to travel to 109n

Chaucer, appalling spelling of 67n
Shakespeare:
    appalling spelling and grammar of 90
    also quite a lot doesn't make much sense in author's opinion 90
    although greatest man to have ever been born, probably 89
Stevenson, Juliet:
    greatest Shakespeare actress of this century 90
    close personal acquaintance with author of 89
Zhivago:
    legendary role of Omar Sharif and greatest film ever made, in my opinion, bar Ben Hur and Khartoum 22n

: 50 :

Guess who?

In *Honeytrap: The Secret Worlds of Stephen Ward* by A. Summers and
S. Dorril (Weidenfeld & Nicolson, 1987), an account of the John
Profumo / Christine Keeler political and high-life London scandal
of the 1960s, great care has been taken to avoid libellous assertion,
by the simple expedient of omitting the names of eleven people fea-
tured in the text. They are replaced by long dashes and asterisks
leading to footnotes reading, in ten cases, 'Name deleted for legal
reasons', and in one, 'Name deleted for personal security'. This gave
rise to difficulties of alphabetization in the index, solved by listing
all eleven under:

> anonymous:
> — Lord ('sinister bisexual'), 121
> — (friend of Lord Astor), 161
> — (Hungarian woman), 191
> — (lesbians), 149, 217
> — (former MI6 operative), 151-3
> — (minister who offered to resign), 4, 209
> — (model), 54
> — (Conservative MP), 118, 133, 212
> — (member of the Royal Family), 211
> — (Conservative Secretary of State), 213
> — (solicitor), 209

Political affiliation no secret

For sheer, over-the-top attack, here are a few of the 140 subheadings under Reagan, Ronald Wilson in *The Clothes Have no Emperor: A Chronicle of the Reagan Years* by Paul Slansky (Fireside Books, Simon & Schuster, 1989). The indexer was clearly no admirer of the Republican leader.

> blames Carter
> blames Congress
> blames the media
> blames miscellaneous others
> cancerous pimple called 'friend' by
> challenge to accuracy of [18 page references]
> confusion admitted by
> correction issued by or on behalf of
> cues taken by
> detachment from reality imputed to
> disbelief by public of
> gloating by enemies of
> improbable letters of support cited by
> inability to answer questions of [19 page references]
> macho bluster of [17 page references]
> misstatements by [33 page references]
> mistakes admitted and not admitted by
> provokes unintended laughter
> unawareness of
> the waking or non-waking of

Nudge, nudge

The index to Julian Barnes's *Letters from London 1990-1995* (Picador, 1995) received special mention in the *Sunday Telegraph*: 'the index alone is so funny that it's worth the cover price of the book.' It appears full of private jokes and private feuds, indulged by classification as well as by choice of terms.

Letters from London reproduces Barnes' reports as London correspondent to the *New Yorker*, political and partial. He is a supremely witty writer in several genres, and has employed particular techniques here to produce an index of high comedy.

Barnes has contrived his index entries from passages of text most cleverly and selectively. One essay opens:

> Last month I took part in a fund-raiser for a cash-strapped Oxford college: two poets, two prose writers and two musicians were the evening's entertainment. ... The organizer began by apologizing for the fact that my advertised fellow-novelist was at the last minute unavoidably unable to make it (he had unavoidably gone skiing, but the fictioneers' free-masonry does not permit me to finger him).

Indeed, anonymity is at this point preserved. But, resorting to the index, we find an entry with one sole reference:

McEwan, Ian: unavoidably goes skiing

In an article on the World Chess Championship, Barnes frequently quotes Cathy Forbes' biography, *Nigel Short: Quest for the Crown*. Among the items gleaned from it is that Short's coach 'also pays attention to the regulation of his charge's bodily functions. After Short has let off steam by playing his guitar before a game, Kavalek will remind him to empty his bladder.'

This leads to the index entry for the author – with no mention of the biography –

Forbes, Cathy: urinary pattern of Nigel Short

The following text: 'Poet Laureate Ted Hughes obliged with [as a special Election Day poem] a jocose number about the effect of toxic chemicals on the sperm count of Western males,' is précised in the text as:

Hughes, Ted: gonadic appeal

Of Margaret Thatcher's memoirs, *The Downing Street Years*, Barnes notes omissions from the index that he finds significant, including 'the name of a British subject sentenced to death by a foreign power during her premiership. ... Bad luck, Citizen Rushdie.' So, in Barnes's book's index:

Rushdie, Salman: plight fails to stir Mrs Thatcher

Barnes' own opinions are shrewdly reinforced in the index, in truly partial style:

The British have managed to export some surprising things – cricket, marmalade, the humour of Benny Hill –

yields, in the index:

Hill, Benny, mysterious exportability of

Tracing the course of the 1992 General Election, Barnes lets fall: 'Not even Andrew Lloyd Webber's threat to leave the country in the event of a Labour victory had persuaded enough people to vote for Neil Kinnock.' Salt is rubbed into the wound in the index:

Lloyd Webber, Andrew: threat to leave the country if Labour elected fails to make enough people vote Labour

Barnes does not care for Lady Thatcher. A column-long entry following her name includes:

rumours of lunacy; receives electric shocks in bath; 'bawls like a fishwife'; accused of war crimes; new version of St Augustine; how not to make the poor richer; discovers it's a funny old world; compared to Hamlet's father; compared to Catherine the Great; bursts into flame; omnipresence; effect on carol singers; unimpressed by the French Revolution

For some entries in this index, it is the straight-faced lack of comment that enchants:

Bruno, Frank: almost hurts Mike Tyson; stars in Aladdin
Heseltine, Michael: a rich blonde
Kasparov, Gary: psychological bruiser
Lloyd's of London: 'HIV of the upper-middle classes'

Philip, Prince, Duke of Edinburgh: given to ducal gaffes; whispered
  mistresses
Ridley, Nicholas: assorted gaffes

Other entries tell their own sad tale:

Howe, Sir Geoffrey: loyal Thatcherite; sacked by Mrs Thatcher; very
  dull; disloyal Thatcherite; biting doormat; booted around by European colleagues
Major, John: not renowned for flair; makes a joke; denounced as dull;
  satirist's nemesis; dwindling allure
Meyer, Sir Anthony: sacrificial rabbit, twittering canary or stalking-
  horse?
Trelford, Donald: condemns stories about Royals; prints story about
  Royals

Classification leads to some splendidly cumulative index paragraphs, such as:

Alcohol: Liebfraumilch and Ron Brown MP; champagne and Ron
  Brown MP; sparkling wine and Ron Brown MP
Animals: Mrs Thatcher as she-elephant; Geoffrey Howe as rabbit;
  Geoffrey Howe as Rottweiler in drag; Michael Heseltine as hornet
Brown, Ron, MP: parliamentary record; sexual record; criminal
  record
sheep: Geoffrey Howe; Andrew Neil; Lloyd's investors

A delightful index indeed. Nevertheless, one would not rest content with reading only the index, despite the comment by the *Sunday
Telegraph*. After reading these subheadings under 'sex', who could
refrain from turning to the pages cited?

lesbian panto; the case of Nona's knickers; and the Royal Family;
Britannia's bra size; Claudia Schiffer's satanic breasts; Duke of
Edinburgh; British taste for sodomy; how the English achieve preg-
nancy; Tony Blair

: 53 :
No fury like it

A Slight and Delicate Creature, the self-titled memoirs of Margaret Cook (Weidenfeld & Nicolson, 1999) was written shortly after the lady's husband, the then British Foreign Secretary, had left her for a younger woman, in a blaze of publicity and vehement denunciation. Notoriously, Mrs Cook attacked her former mate throughout the media, not excepting even the index to her book. It includes in the entry for the errant husband, Robin Cook, the wifely-eye sub-headings:

> outbursts of temper
> and guilt transference
> heavy drinking
> weight problems
> sexual difficulties

> *Indexes need not necessarily be dry, and in some cases*
> *they form the most interesting portion of a book*
> H.B. Wheatley, *What is an Index?* 1878

Inveighing against the computer

Clifford Stoll's trenchant volume, *High-tech Heretic: Why Computers Don't Belong in the Classroom and Other Reflections by a Computer Contrarian* (Doubleday, 1999) is described on the cover as 'a thorough detonation of the hype surrounding computers in our lives'. With the author's encouragement, the indexer of the book, Nancy Mulvany, carried the denunciations through to the index – which is headed, 'Index with an Attitude', and includes these entries:

Addictive nature of the Internet
Attention deficit syndrome,
    encouraged by technology
Barbarians, invasion of teaching
    by
Blandness and brevity
    multimedia writing style
    See also Educational dullness
Community
    disengagement from
    undermining of
Curriculum development
    anti-intellectual design of
Customers as software guinea pigs
Dumbing down of schools, chal-
    lenging topics dodged
Educational dullness
    See also Blandness and brevity;
      Intellectual passivity; Nation
      of dolts
Empty promises, of the past
Hack writing for multimedia

Information is free, not really
Information is power, not really
Junk food analogy
Macintosh computer, as aquarium
Nation of dolts
    educational dullness
    how to create
Planned obsolescence
Pleasing the indexer, a good idea
    [an in-joke!]
Presentation software as enemy of
    a good talk
Sandbox replaced by computers
Third-rate education. *See* Dis-
    tance learning
Ugly computers
Writing
    blandness and brevity, the new
      style
    cranking out info-nuggets
    to please the indexer

21st century

: 55 :

Invecticon

Lexicon of Musical Invective by Nicolas Slonimsky (W.W. Norton & Co., 2000), arranged alphabetically by composer, quotes prolifically from 'biased, unfair, ill-tempered, and singularly unprophetic judgments' which the editor has culled from the musical files of the past. Instead of an index, this anthology of 'critical assaults' upon composers – from Beethoven through Stravinsky – has an aptly named 'Invecticon,' in which composers are referenced by the insulting adjectives that have been heaped upon them in the reviews collected between these covers. For example:

> Pigs (grunting of) Strauss, 193
> Pigs (ringed) Schoenberg, 156
> Pitiful insanity, Milhaud, 124
> Plague of insects, Rachmaninoff, 137

Indexer manqué

The email edition of the *Bangkok Post Week in Review* for 24-30 September 2000 – 'A review of what made news in Thailand, the region and All The Rest Of The World during the past week' – has the following paragraph headings about Thaksin Shinawatra, leader of the Thai Rak Thai political party:

> Thaksin cited
> Thaksin sighted
> Thaksin slighted
> Thaksin sited

The paragraphs refer, respectively, to Mr Thaksin's being investigated for corruption, attempting to avoid the media, his reputation, and references to him on Web sites. Clearly the editor is an indexer *manqué*.

: 57 :

Look, you

Frewin Poffley's *Greek Island Hopping* (Thomas Cook Publishing, 2001) has as the only entry in its index under U:

> U will find the only 'u's in Greece are sheep

: II :

FICTION AND VERSE WITH
INDEXES

Although by no means standard practice, serious novels may be indexed in the same way as biographies or histories, as narratives concerning groups of people and the events in their lives that readers may well wish to find again. Surely fiction that is serious, lengthy and complex is at least as deserving of these aids to study and research as any other form of writing. Jane Austen's novels, *Pilgrim's Progress*, Orwell's *1984*, Scott's Waverley novels, Tolkien's *The Lord of the Ring*, Tolstoy's *Resurrection*, have all appeared with indexes; as have Proust's *A La Recherche du Temps Perdu* and Balzac's *La Comédie Humaine*.

Anthony Raven, the indexer of the Pavilion 1982 edition of Jerome K. Jerome's *Three Men in a Boat*, argued on this issue:[1]

> The facts in a work of fiction may have no independent existence outside it, whereas those in a work of non-fiction do exist independently of the book, but that is irrelevant. Within the context of the book, which is all an index is concerned with ... all facts are equally factual, and indexable, regardless of whether they also enjoy a different kind of factuality beyond the book's covers. ... book indexes index books, not real life.

Hans Wellisch regretted, 'only about a dozen or so indexes to fictional works are known to have been compiled from the mid-18th to the early 20th century', and urged the need for them:[2]

> Novels such as *Don Quixote, War and Peace, The Magic Mountain* and *Gone With the Wind*, to name only a few mighty tomes with dozens or even hundreds of characters, places, and events, lack indexes, and many other classical as well as lesser known but voluminous and complex novels would also benefit from them. ... many readers, particularly students ... may wish to return to a passage in which a certain character appears, but find it difficult to do so for want of an index.

Indexes to novels, though, may not always be of wholly serious intent, and in most of those quoted here the authors have seized the opportunity for further fun, and even to devise new literary forms. Judy Batchelor, in a review article[3] discussing two novels with indexes (see nos. 13 and 14 below), deemed one of these 'a *para-index*, a guide not to the overt topics but to its subtext and its personal connotations', and commented, 'On the whole, the index is more entertainment than use – but so, after all, is a novel'. Her article ended, 'Innovation in indexing is powerfully to be encouraged; the non-index and the sub-index have been with us for many years, and we may now perhaps look forward to the meta-index, the *sur*-index and who knows what further developments.'

Verse, too, occasionally attracts subject indexing – most often, it appears from the examples here, for humorous purposes.

1 Anthony Raven, 'Indexes to works of fiction' (letter). *The Indexer* vol. 17 (1) April 1990, pp 60-61
2 Hans Wellisch. *Indexing from A to Z,* H. W. Wilson 1995, pp 181-3
3 Judy Batchelor, 'Para-index and anti-index'. *The Indexer* vol. 16 (3) April 1989, p 194

: I :

18th-century vindictive

The Dunciad is a long (1,754-line) satirical poem on Dullness, written by Alexander Pope and first published in 1728. It includes an eccentric critical apparatus by an invented critic: eleven pages of preface and prelims, copious footnotes, nine pages of appendices, a two-page 'Index of persons celebrated in this poem' and five-page 'Index of matters contained in this poem and notes'. The second index also contains references to another work, *The Testimonies of Authors concerning our Poet and his Works*, published by Pope under the name of Martinus Scriblerus.

The indexes are alphabetized by first letter only, all entries that begin with the same letter simply being subsumed in the same section, not further ordered by alphabetical sequence. I and J appear together (as, in order, Index-Learning, Journals, Jus, Impudence), as do U and V (Verbal, Venice, University, UPTON).

The entries below, taken from the second index, show how the attacks in the poem and *Testimonies* upon Pope's critics, whom he regarded as bitter enemies, are there carried through and reinforced. They remain in the original order of their appearance. Capital letters and square brackets are given as in the original; double brackets indicate our own editorial interpolations.

Anger, one of the characteristics of Mr Dennis's critical writings
—Affirmation, another
[To which are added by Mr Theobald, Ill-nature, Spite, Revenge]
BLACKMORE (Sir Richard), his Impiety and Irreligion, proved by Mr Dennis
—His abuse of Mr Dryden and Mr Pope
Bray, a word much beloved by Sir Richard

Booksellers, how they run for a Poet
Bailiffs, how poets run from them
CIBBER, Hero of the Poem ... not absolutely stupid ... His folly heightened with Frenzy ... He was once thought to have wrote a reasonable Play ... Finally subsides in the lap of Dulness, where he rests to all eternity ((an entry of 41 lines, run-on))
CURL (Edm.), his Panegyric

: 2 :

'The bliss of excessive fondness'

Dr Samuel Johnson suggested to his friend Samuel Richardson, in a letter of 1753, 'the propriety of making an index to his novels, *Clarissa, Pamela*, and *Sir Charles Grandison*, that 'when the reader recollects any incident, he may easily find it'.

Some twenty years later, Johnson observed to his friend Boswell, 'Why, Sir, if you were to read Richardson for the story, your impatience would be so much fretted that you would hang yourself. But you must read him for the sentiment, and consider the story as only giving occasion to the sentiment'. Perhaps we have here the reason for the first index to English works of fiction, and its peculiar (to us) principle of selection of items to index.

Richardson compiled an *index Rerum* (of topics) to *Clarissa* in 1751, and in 1754 provided for *Sir Charles Grandison* an 'Index Historical and Characteristical of the Seven Volumes of this Work'. In 1755 he published as a separate work of 450 pages, *A Collection of Such of the Moral and Instructive Sentiments, Maxims, Cautions and Reflexions, Contained in the Histories of Pamela, Clarissa, and Sir Charles Grandison*, described in the Preface as a 'General Index both of Maxims and Reflections'. Entries are listed in sections, the section headings in alphabetical order, such as Learning. Libertine. / Rake. Wit. Writers. Youth. A specimen section from the index to *Clarissa* is:

Learning.
> A LETTER'D education too generally sets the children of the poor above those servile offices, by which the business of the world is carried on, iii. 363 [iv.148]
>
> Take the world thro' there are twenty happy people among the unletter'd, to one among those who have had a school-education, iii. 364 [iv. 148]
>
> Yet who would not wish to lift to some little distinction and gentle usefulness, the person he desires to reward? *ibid.*
>
> The little words in the Republic of Letters, like the little folks in a nation, are the most useful and significant, iv. 82 [275]
>
> A man of the deepest Learning may hear something from even a mean preacher that he knew not before, or at least that he had not considered in the same light, iv. 125 [322]

> The early Learning of women, which chiefly consists in what they pick up from inflaming Novels, and improbable Romances, contributes greatly to enervate and weaken their minds, vi. 334. [vii. 261]

Isaac D'Israeli (who lived 1776-1848) expressed the most derogatory views of such indexing by an author of his own fictional works. They appear in his essay, 'Richardson', in *Curiosities of Literature*, published in three volumes by Frederick Warne & Co. (undated; vol. 2, pp 62-5), as follows:

> He was delighted by his own works. No author enjoyed so much the bliss of excessive fondness. ... The extreme delight which he felt on a review of his own works the works themselves witness. Each is an evidence of what some will deem a violent literary vanity. ... To the author's own edition of his *Clarissa* is appended an *alphabetical arrangement* of the sentiments displayed throughout the work; and such was the fondness that dictated this voluminous arrangement, that such trivial aphorisms as, "habits are not easily changed," "men are known by their companions," &c., seem alike to be the object of their author's admiration. This collection of sentiments, said indeed to have been sent to him anonymously, is curious and useful, and shows the value of the work, by the extensive grasp of that mind which could think so justly on such numerous topics. And in his third and final labour, to each volume of *Sir Charles Grandison* is not only prefixed a complete *index*, with as much exactness as if it were a History of England, but there is also appended a *list* of the *similes* and allusions in the volume; some of which do not exceed *three* or *four* in nearly as many hundred pages.
>
> Literary history does not record a more singular example of that self-delight which an author has felt on a revision of his works. It was this intense pleasure which produced his voluminous labours. It must be confessed that there are readers deficient in that sort of genius which makes the mind of Richardson so fertile and prodigal.

So – the indexing of fiction did not get off to a good start, historically.

Hymnal half-lines

Ira D. Sankey's *Sacred Songs and Solos* of 1873 includes an index entry for the hymn, 'There is a land mine eyes have seen':

'There is a land mine'

Another old hymn book entry is reputed to run:

'O Lord, what boots'

to indicate the hymn beginning:

'O Lord, what boots it to recall / The hours of anguish spent'

So essential did I consider an index to be to every book, that I proposed to bring a Bill into Parliament to deprive an author who publishes a book without an index of the privilege of copyright, and, moreover, to subject him for his offence to a pecuniary penalty.

Lord Chief Justice Campbell,
Lives of the Chief Justices of England Vol. III, Preface (1846)

: 4 :

Victorian whimsicality

In at least one of his works, *Sylvie and Bruno,* Lewis Carroll showed that he had mastered the art of indexing, Victorian style. The first part of *Sylvie and Bruno* was published in 1889 by Macmillan, with an index whose whimsicality perfectly fitted the equally whimsical text, though it occupied only five of the book's 400 pages. Four years later, there appeared *Sylvie and Bruno concluded,* and this time Carroll provided it with a 'General index' of 21 pages which included most of the entries for volume I as well as entries for volume II.

In both versions of the index double, triple and even fourfold entries abound, such as:

> Boots for Horizontal Weather
> Horizontal rain, boots for
> Weather, horizontal, boots for
>
> Bread-sauce appropriate for Weltering
> Weltering, appropriate fluids for
>
> Crocodiles, logic of
> Logic of Crocodiles
> Onus probandi, misplaced by Crocodiles
> Proof, burden of, misplaced by Crocodiles

Other gems from this index are:

> Artistic effect said to require indistinctiveness
> Asylums, Lunatic-, future use for
> Bath, portable, for Tourists
> Croquet. Why is it demoralizing?
> Experimental honeymoons
> Fairies, how to improve character of
>   "   "   " recognize presence of
> Frog, young, how to amuse
> Horses, Runaway, how to control
> Life, Future, what interest will survive in it?
> Life, how to enjoy
>   in falling house
>   in reversed order

purpose of, as viewed by Child
regarded as a Drama
Man, advantage of, over the Dog
Men, little, privileges of
Playing for money, a moral act
Reason, power of, in Dog
Scenery, enjoyment of, by little men
Sinfulness, amount of, in World
Spherical, advantage of being
Walking sticks that walk alone, how to obtain
Water, people lighter than, how to obtain

These two novels by Carroll differ from his other fiction in a number of ways beside having their own indexes. Each of them, for example, is several times as long as either of the Alice books; but more importantly, the Sylvie and Bruno books were written with a moral – something studiously avoided in the Alice books and almost all of Carroll's other fiction written during his adult years. Amid the comic entries in Carroll's index we find the following references to serious subjects seriously discussed:

'Doing good,' ambiguity of the phrase
Loving or being loved, Which is best?
Paley's definition of virtue
Spencer, Herbert, difficulties in

Sadly, when the *Sylvie and Bruno* books have been reprinted in the one-volume tomes purporting to be 'The Complete Works of Lewis Carroll', the indexes to *Sylvie and Bruno* are regularly omitted. Presumably the publishers either do not appreciate their importance and novelty, or do not wish to incur the expense of adjusting the page references.

A.A.I. / H.H.W.

Transindexuality

Virginia Woolf's fictional biography, *Orlando* (Hogarth Press, 1928) devotes two pages out of 299 to an index listing characters, and titles of literary works. Woolf's playfulness about *Orlando*'s category met difficulties; booksellers, confused by its apparent status as biography, as indicated on the title page, and supported by its possession of an index, refused to sell it as fiction. Leon Edel, in *Writing Lives, Principia Biographica* writes of *Orlando*: 'In keeping with its nature the volume is endowed with an index. The pretence of scholarship and exactitude is maintained to the end'.

The entry for the main character, Orlando, who lives for 400 years and during this lifetime turns from man to woman, duly changes sex half-way through, thus, from:

> Orlando, appearance as a boy, 15; writes his first play, 16; visits Queen at Whitehall, 24; made Treasurer and Steward, 25; ...

through to —

> ... confused with her cousin, 220; returns to her country house, 233; breaks her ankle, 248; declared a woman, 255; engagement, 250; marriage, 264; birth of her first son, 295

: 6 :

Verse, bad – index, good

The Stuffed Owl is an avowed 'Anthology of Bad Verse' – though none of its items was intended by its author to be deemed as such. It was compiled, prefaced, hilariously annotated, sub-titled and indexed by D. B. Wyndham Lewis and Charles Lee. The authors write in their preface:

> Bad Verse has its canons, like Good Verse. ... good Bad Verse has an eerie, supernatural beauty comparable in its accidents with the beauty of Good Verse. ... good Bad Verse is devilish pleasing. ... it is generally the most distinguished poets who provide the nicest Bad Verse ... men and women to whom Almighty God in his inscrutable providence has seen fit to deny a sense of humour.

The Stuffed Owl was first published (by J. M. Dent) in January 1930, and followed swiftly in the same year by a revised and enlarged edition, with a note ending: 'It is hoped that serious students will welcome the addition of a Subject Index.'

All the index entries are perfectly valid, some object-lessons in subject-headings for brevity and perception. To help connoisseurs identify the original poems, the authors are added in parenthesis to all the index entries quoted here. Turning to the original poems and learning what gave rise to the entries is sheer joy.

Angels, not immune from curiosity; give Mr. Purcell a flying lesson; patrol the British sky; invited to take up permanent quarters at Whitehall; & Britons, mixed choir of, ibid. (Dryden, Pollock, Sheffield, Watts, Watts, Watts)

Ankles, oedematous, S. Lee's (Wordsworth)

Arden, Enoch, his expensive obsequies, his early married life, (Tennyson)

Bates, charming Mr. (Watts)

Botanist, as mountaineer, inferior to goat (Shenstone)

Byron, Lord, believed to be a poet; his low character; his career sketched in a few bold strokes (Julia Moore)

Christians, liable to leak (Balmford)

Cow, attention drawn to, by Tradition (Bloomfield)

Eggs, mention of, wrapped in elegant obscurity (Armstrong)

England, small but well-known; emphatically undegenerate (Eliza Cook)

Fish, Tennyson contrives to avoid mentioning

'Flash! bang!'subtly varied with

'Bang! flash!' (q.v.) (Gordon)

Gabriel, the Archangel, titivates himself (Cowley)

George II, his particularly nice virtues; his half-share in the universe; his fortunate philoprogenitiveness; his blooming honours; his godlike appearance, ibid. (Eusden, Cibber, Young)

German place-names, the poet does his best with (Cibber)

Gill, Harry, his extensive but inadequate wardrobe (Wordsworth)

Grave, living, see Shark; rose-covered; suicide's, rendezvous at a; mother's, habit of dancing on, reprobated (Turner, Whur, Warton, Dobell)

Guardian Angel, Miss Jewsbury's, has a pressing engagement (Wordsworth)

Handkerchiefs, relays of, called for (Anon.)

Heaven, system of book-keeping in; vogue of Mr. Purcell's music in; unexpected grandeur of its architecture; knowledge of languages useful in, ibid.; blasted; haloes the only wear in (Dryden, Sheffield, Watts, E. B. Browning, Close)

Immortality, hope of, distinguishes man from silk-worm (Wordsworth)

Italy, not recommended to tourists; examples of what goes on there (Della Cruseans, Carter, Lytton, Lytton)

Jessy, succumbs to Henry's wiles; chased by birds and lambs; reproved by jasmines, ibid.; cut by neighbours, ibid.; embarks for unspecified destination; last seen floating on watery plain, ibid. (Shenstone)

Leeds, poetical aspects of (Dyer)

Lewdness, lax-eyed, lustful sons of (Dobell)

Liverpool, rapture experienced at (Baker)

Maiden, Swiss, coming-on disposition of (Longfellow)

Mansion, heavenly, kept vacant for the Warner family (Watts)

Mead, awful Mr. (Watts)

Mechanic, pale, exhibited in a hurry to wallow in vice (White)

Milk, periphrastically indicated (Armstrong, Jerningham)

Monster, grim, awful behaviour of (Whur)

Moon, See Dorsal region, lunar

Muse, reformed by a pension; invited to celebrate Mr. Baker's return to health; proves unequal to the task (Young, Chatterton)

Nature, her sins commensurate with her size; a coy and aged virgin; run to earth by Dr. Harvey (Cowley)

Negroes, liable to worms; prone to bloat, ibid.; their nails often found in Christmas puddings (Grainger, Smart)

Newt, trustworthy (Eliza Cook)

Norns, reboantic (Chivers)

Oysters, reason why they cannot be crossed in love (Darwin, E.)

Pea, not self-supporting (Bidlake)

Pond, 3ft. x 2ft. (Wordsworth)

Silk-worm, Spartan tastes of; sinks into hopeless grave (Wordsworth)

Surprise, vain, Samson's; immense, Mr. Gunstone's; unqualified, Jonah's; (Anon., Watts, Young)

Tapeworm, lonely but prolific (E. Darwin)

Tears, telescopic; examples of their use in sundry emergencies; miscellaneous ... (Watts, Byron)

Trains, rapture of catching; used indiscriminately by all ranks (Baker)

Wamer, Mrs., goes house-hunting in heaven (Watts)

Washing, cautiously recommended (Armstrong)

Wet-nurses, male parents useless as (Wordsworth)

William III, his royal breath repaired; escorted from Torbay by brigades of angels (Shadwell, Watts)

Wives, should wash occasionally; a modicum of intelligence desirable in; but not too much (Armstrong, Whur, Tupper)

Woman, useful as a protection against lions (Merry)

Workhouse, impassioned invitation to the (Dyer)

Worm, lisping; militant; farfetched, *see* Silk-worm (hymns)

Yams, conflict of authorities concerning (Grainger)

Yarker, Mr., his lamented dropping off (Close)

York, Duke of, a cargo in himself (Dryden)

We have long been disposed to join that grateful gentleman who always puts up a special prayer for dictionary and index makers. It is indeed the only reward which the latter obtain, for their severe toil rarely meets a sufficient pecuniary recompense, and their names are forgotten even by those who profit from their labours.

The Englishman and Military Chronicle
(Calcutta, 13 March 1851)

Misleading indexes

A. P. Herbert provided humorous indexes to his humorous legal books, collections of imaginary court cases. Since none of these was ever heard in any actual court of law, they may be accounted works of fiction.

Take, for example, the following tantalising and provocative extract from *Uncommon Law* (Methuen, 1935):

DRAINS: need not be attended to, at the House of Commons

EUROPA: shocking allegations

FISH-PORTERS: said to suffer little hardship through high cost of libel actions

Hamlet: counts as a dog-race

HIPPOPOTAMUS: compared with Divorce Laws

IMMORAL EARNINGS: *see* Post Office

MARRIAGE

Admirals, denied benefits of, by inequitable treatment

Naval officers lured into, on false pretences

Not, legally, the same as slavery

Touching belief of Charlotte Watts in delights of

The *Hamlet* entry, for instance, refers to the following passage in the text: '"Entertainment" includes any exhibition, performance, amusement, game, or sport to which persons are admitted for payment, so that in the same wide category are included a performance of *Hamlet* and the racing of dogs, a religious drama and a travelling circus, the fiddling of a Kreisler and the roaring of a caged lion, a game of cricket or a tragedy of Ibsen.'

In spite of the fantastic nature of the entries in A.P.H.'s indexes, reference to the actual text pages shows that there is sound foundation for most of them. For example, these following entries from the index to *Misleading Cases in the Common Law* (1927):

Actresses: Appearance of, inappropriate subject for reflection (*see* "Sunday")

Fun: No authority for the idea that we are here for

Legal Profession: Body and soul, in, difficulty of keeping together

Principle: Definitions (*and see* "Blondes")

The index to *More Misleading Cases* (1927) is packed with amusing entries. 'Haddock' in this book represents Herbert himself.

BANKRUPTCY:
  conspiracy to produce: See
    Inland Revenue
  gradual decline of Haddock
    towards
BLACKMAIL: See Collector of
  Taxes
CRIME, See Income
EDUCATION, ELEMEN-
  TARY:
  distressing manners of many
    children who have enjoyed
    public
  Held—does not necessarily
    include reading, writing and
    arithmetic
  orchards stripped by beneficiar-
    ies of free public

pleasing characteristics of children without
INCOME:
  Christian treatment suggested
    due to earners of,
  earnings of, wrongfully
    regarded as felony
INCOME TAX:
  derision of, lawful
  immoral basis of, exposed
MAGISTRATES:
  conscientious study of obscene
    literature by
  quiet pride of, in freedom from
    classical education
'OY!', USE OF: See Education
REX: persistent litigation of

The index to *Bardot M.P. and Other Misleading Cases* (Methuen, 1930) is elaborate and detailed, comprising 44 columns to 194 pages of text. The more riotous entries include:

AUTHORS:
  barbarously used in life; in
    death
  generous natures abused
  get nothing out of Arts Council
  sacrificed to Privileged
    Libraries
COMPUTERS:
  a menace, accurate or not
COST OF LIVING:
  M. P.'s responsibility for inex-
    cusable items in
PASSPORTERY: absconding
  scientists easily evade
  communists untroubled by
  cosmic vexation through
  criminals laugh heartily at

SPLIT PERSONALITY causes
  consecutive terms of impris-
    onment
  causes two convictions
  held, does not excuse bigamy
STATUTORY ROBBERY, *see*
  'Copyright Libraries'
'SUMMER TIME':
  described as 'shameful'
  double, deprecated
  perpetual, apprehended
'TAX ADVANTAGE':
  bestial pursuit of, thwarted
  teetotallers' shameless enjoy-
    ment of

R.L.W.C.

A clerihindex?

The Complete Clerihews of E. Clerihew Bentley has an index as original as its content. A 'clerihew' is described in the introduction by Gavin Ewart as 'a humorous pseudo-biographical quatrain, rhymed as two couplets, with lines of uneven length', giving the example:

> Sir Christopher Wren
> Said, 'I am going to dine with some men.
> If anybody calls,
> Say I am designing St Paul's.'

The clerihews have been published in a succession of volumes, each with its own index (the work of Bentley himself). The first composite index, selective only, was to *Clerihews Complete* (1951). *The Complete Clerihews* (O.U.P., 1981), was the first complete collection published, succeeded in 1983 by a revised, paperback edition, including for the first time all entries from all the original indexes.

There are 140 verses in the 1983 volume, provided with an index of ten pages, double-column, headed:

> Index of Psychology, Mentality and Other Things frequently noted in connection with genius.

The index cites merely the subjects of the verses instead of page numbers; the verses are printed in alphabetical order of subjects' names – one to a page, illustrated. The quatrain quoted above yields a reference under each letter of the alphabet; a proportion of index to text of more than 650%!

These are some sample entries from this most unusual and attractive, thoroughly interpretative index.

action, prompt and decisive,
  unfitness for position requiring
  (OTTO)
agitation, reluctance to explain
  (BEIT)
atrocity (WREN)

bankruptcy, moral (WREN)
Bellona, embraces of, narrow
  escape from (SHAW)
blessedness, single, undervaluation of (HENRY VIII)
blood, heyday in the, inability to

tame (BEDE, HENRY VIII);
Norman, capacity to lose
(RUFUS)

bowl, the, disinclination to shun
(DANTE, POINCARÉ)

cheering, loud and prolonged,
during which the honourable
gentleman did not resume his
seat (COMTE)

conduct, disingenuous (WREN)

contretemps, awkward, liability to
(HENRY VIII, ODO, SNOW-
DEN)

domesticity (HENRY VIII,
IBSEN)

domestic servants, dishonesty
among, encouragement of
(WREN)

done, simply not, repugnance to
what is (PEEL, STUBBS)

escutcheon, blot on, action involv-
ing (WREN)

fact, cynical perversion of
(WREN)

frequency, nuptial (HENRY
VIII)

gametomania (HENRY VIII)

glamour, negative reaction to
(KNOX)

guile (WREN)

habits, repugnant personal, often
found in association with fine
spiritual gifts (BUNYAN)

hypocrisy, calculated (WREN)

integrity, low standard of
(WREN)

Jesuitical dealing (WREN)

knavery (WREN)

lie, bouncing circulation of
(WREN)

Machiavelli, unholy precepts of,
tendency to act upon (WREN)

mercy, bowels of, non-equipment
with (TORQUEMADA)

monogamy, recurrent (HENRY
VIII)

noblesse oblige, disregard of
apothegm (WREN)

openness, want of (CANUTE,
WREN)

principle, lack of (WREN)

queenhood, lavishness in the matter of (HENRY VIII)

quickening, spiritual, need of
(WREN)

Restoration, lax morality of,
readiness to fall in with
(WREN)

Satanism, revolting display of
(WREN)

temperament, artistic, the: its
acute sensitiveness (VAN
EYCK); deliberate eccentricity
(FIFE); drunkenness (ERAS-
MUS); high value set upon it
by Frenchmen (TIZIANO);
irresistibly attracted by the sublime (GRIEG); love of violent
action (LISZT); naive self-
appreciation (CIMABUE)

turpitude (WREN)

untruth, plausible, ability to frame
(WREN)

uxory (HENRY VIII, IBSEN)

variety, thirst for (BENN,
HENRY VIII)

veracity, departure from (WREN)

width (HENRY VIII)

wood-notes wild, native, unfair
competition with (SHAKE-
SPEARE)

world, the next, neglect of
prospects in (WREN)

Xmas, failure to merit gifts at
(WREN)

YMCA, unfitness for (WREN)

zealous pursuit of pleasure at
expense of soul (WREN)

Zion, outcast from (WREN)

Editorial usurpation

The index in Vladimir Nabokov's novel, *Pale Fire* (Weidenfeld, 1962) is itself veritable fiction, or a component thereof. This index is the second transforming layer covering – or smothering – or totally transforming – a 999-line autobiographical poem (composed on 80 index cards) by John Shade, an American professor and poet. An *apparatus criticus* surrounds – engulfs – it: a 16-page foreword and 229-page commentary by Charles Kinbote, Shade's neighbour and fellow-lecturer. From these, it becomes apparent that Kinbote is a lunatic who grandiosely fantasises that he is a European ('Zemblan') king, who escaped from revolution in his country; and that Shade was murdered (in a case of mistaken identity) after finishing the poem, while Kinbote madly assumes the bullet to have been intended for his own assassination. The entire commentary reinterprets (distorts the meaning of) the poem, expressing Kinbote's fantasies in the index/glossary, whose entries all refer to his own commentary on the poem rather than to the poem's text. The entry for the editor himself takes two of the index's ten and a half pages, opening with the (wholly misleading) gloss:

> Kinbote, Charles, Dr., an intimate friend of S, his literary advisor, editor and commentator

Shade himself gets just over one page for his index entry.

Kinbote's enemies are disdainfully dismissed in the index, not even named: mentioned in subheadings, the hated 'Prof. C', 'E.' and 'Prof. H.' are each followed only by a parenthesis, '(not in Index)'; while the poet's beloved wife, to whom the poem is addressed throughout, and whom the commentary bitterly denigrates, receives the sole entry:

> Shade, Sybil, S's wife, passim.

Teasing games are played. A theme of the commentary is the failure of the Zemblan rebels to find the crown jewels artfully concealed by Kinbote (King Charles X). The index includes the trail:

Crown Jewels see Hiding Place.
Hiding place, *potaynik* (q.v.)
Potaynik, taynik (q.v.)
Taynik, Russ., secret place; see Crown Jewels.

In the absence of any reference to Zembla and its Royal Family in the poem, their story is recounted wholly in the commentary and index. The index, with the commentary, constitutes Kinbote's own fantasy autobiography, as for example depicted in these entries:

Alfin, King, surnamed The Vague, 1873-1918, reigned from 1900; K.'s father [N. B. 'K' = Kinbote = the editor/indexer himself]; a kind, gentle, absent-minded monarch, mainly interested in automobiles, flying machines, motorboats and, at one time, sea shells; killed in an airplane accident, 71.

Boscobel, site of the Royal Summerhouse, a beautiful, piny and duny spot in W. Zembla, soft hollows imbued with the writer's most amorous recollections; now (1959) a "nudist colony" – whatever that is, 149, 596.

Disa, Duchess of Payn, of Great Payn and Mone; my lovely, pale, melancholy Queen, haunting my dreams, and haunted by dreams of me, b. 1928; her album and favorite trees, 49; married 1949, 80; her letters on ethereal paper with a watermark I cannot make out, her image torturing me in my sleep, 433.

Garh, a farmer's daughter, 149, 433. Also a rosy-cheeked gooseboy found in a country lane, north of Troth, in 1936, only now distinctly recalled by the writer.

Glitterntin, Mt., a splendid mountain in the Bera Range (q. v.); pity I may never climb it again, 149.

Igor II, reigned 1800-1845, a wise and benevolent king, son of Queen Yaruga (*q.v.*) and father of Thurgus III (*q.v.*): a very private section of the picture gallery in the Palace, accessible only to the reigning monarch, but easily broken into through Bower P by an inquisitive pubescent, contained the statues of Igor's four hundred favorite catamites, in pink marble, with inset glass eyes and various touched up details, an outstanding exhibition of verisimilitude and bad art, later presented by K. to an Asiatic potentate.

Kalixhaven, a colorful seaport on the western coast, a few miles north of Blawick (*q.v.*), 171; many pleasant memories.

Kobaltana, a once fashionable mountain resort near the ruins of some old barracks now a cold and desolate spot of difficult access and no importance but still remembered in military families and forest castles, not in the text.

Shadows, the, a regicidal organization which commissioned *Gradus* (*q.v.*) to assassinate the self-banished king; its leader's terrible name cannot be mentioned, even in the Index to the obscure work of a scholar.

Surreal complexity

Georges Perec's large and remarkable novel, *Life: a User's Manual: Fictions* (581 pages; first published in French by Hachette, 1970; translation by David Bellos, Collins Harvill, 1988) is in the encyclopaedic tradition. It is set in a Paris apartment block which is also its hero and symbolic template. Some 80 pages are devoted to endmatter: a plan of the apartment block, a chronology of events, a list of authors quoted, an 'alphabetical checklist' of anecdotes mentioned in the narrative, and a comprehensive index. The index, 58 pages, includes persons, places, literary works and characters, operas, songs, branded goods; real and fictional, peripheral or central to the narrative. The entry for PARIS has 64 undifferentiated general references followed by 19 subsections, three columns, of lovingly detailed subheadings for streets, districts, buildings and more.

The appendices seem like integrated parts of the narrative, so much of which consists in clues, patterns, linkages, quests and resolutions. To follow a character or place through the text via the index, checklist, chronology, is to be led to other people, places and topics; only in this 'second reading' may some of the threads in the tapestry stand out to delineate the pattern.

Perec borrows the work of 20 authors as part of a mathematically determined system of allusions in this book. One is the Surrealist Parisian writer, Raymond Roussel. In chapter 87 a landscape in the drawing-room of the hero (who shows resemblances to Roussel) is called *L'Ile mystérieuse* (the title of one of Roussel's favourite novels by Jules Verne), and signed L.N. Montalescot. This name comprises 'a yoking together of the siblings Louise and Norbert, architects of Roussel's most notorious Surrealist construction, a whalebone statue on rails made of calves' lungs' (in Roussel's *Impressions d'Afrique*). In the index of *Life: a User's Manual* Montalescot's dates are given as 1877-1933 – the dates of Roussel's birth and death.

There is even an indexer in this fiction of Perec's: see below, page 145.

J.L.B.

First and last lines

An index of first lines has long been recognized as essential to any anthology or volume of collected poems, but Ogden Nash is perhaps the only author whose work has been embellished with an index of *last* lines. It is tempting to see this as an expression of the deliberate quirkiness of his verse; but the evidence seems to indicate that it was the idea not of the author but of his editors.

It seems that most of his numerous volumes of verse had no index at all; two had conventional indexes of first lines. Scarecrow Press published a Keyword-out-of-context *Index to the Poems of Ogden Nash* by Lavonne Axford, using augmented titles, 1972. Unlike some other such labours of love, it must have been fun to compile.

The index of *last* lines appears in a volume published in the US the year after Nash's death: *I Wouldn't Have Missed It: Selected Poems*, edited by Linell Smith and Isabel Eberstadt (1975), and also in paperback in England as *Candy is Dandy: The Best of Ogden Nash* (Methuen, 1985). Whether this unusual index serves any practical purpose is for more fervent devotees of Ogden Nash to decide; but it may certainly claim to be a whetter of appetites and a stimulator of flagging interest. Such lines from the index as these may well send readers burrowing back into the main text to find out what can possibly have preceded them.

> A wet dog is the lovingest.
> And I certainly wish that either I were more like them or they were less so.
> And Shelley went around pulling doors marked PUSH and pushing doors marked PULL just like everybody else.
> And Zeus said, Yes, I'm an atheist.
> But that gook I won't gobble.
> If I were thou, I'd call me Us.
> One end is moo, the other, milk.
> Their universe wobbles.

J.A.V.

The subject elusive: anti-index

Malcolm Bradbury's novel, *My Strange Quest for Mensonge* (Deutsch, 1987) concerns Henri Mensonge, 'the neglected Structuralist master ... [who] could fairly be called the Structuralist's Structuralist ... in typical Structuralist fashion, Mensonge insists that his subject is not his subject at all. ... Structuralism has taught us the lesson of the "death of the subject",' Bradbury tells us. Or, as Judy Batchelor put it, 'Mensonge has brought the Negation of Being to its logical conclusion by probably never existing ... the index is an *anti-index*, in which the signifier refuses absolutely to relate to the signified. All the page-references are incorrect – how could they not be?' But, she adds, 'The index makes jolly reading in its own right'. Entries include:

Bardot, Brigitte, non-relationship with M. of, 41 [no reference to this non-incident on page 41]
Sameness, *see* Difference
Nouvelle cuisine, contrasted with food, 23; compared with Mondrian, 27
I, is there 1; 38-47

My Strange Quest for Mensonge is also furnished with an anti-bibliography with a final entry reading:

Yves Zylot, *Fin*, Paris, PUF, 1975

J.L.B.

Para-index

Lucy Ellmann's novel, *Sweet Desserts* (Virago, 1988) is the story of two sisters, one the narrator and indexer. The index may be taken as a (comic) extension of the text rather than a locational adjunct. Judy Batchelor wrote, it is 'a guide not to the overt topics but to its sub-text and its personal connotations. The main events and characters are not indexed. It includes self-memos; entries with comments but without page-numbers; entries with no direct reference to the text at all. Other imperatives are added to the normal index's *see*. The index is more entertainment than use; but so, after all, is a novel.'

Some entertaining entries from this index are:

Abstinence, *passim*

Adroitness, my moments of, 57, 96

Aloofness, *see* inhabitants of the British Isles

Aplomb, my total lack of social, 103. And yet, *see also* my moments of adroitness

Automation., *see* autonomy, Chance, and Desertion. *Read* phone-book

Boyfriends, Franny's hand-me-down. *see* less of

Cat, unforeseen responsibilities relating to ownership of a, 115

Chance, 35, 70; *see also* automation; *see also* genetics; *see also* inherited silver souvenir spoons; *see also* luck. In fact, *check* resilience – if worn out, renew

Divorce, *cut* your losses and *go* to Las Vegas

Exile, *passim*

Found objects, *keep*

Happenings, *check* your filofax

Indeterminacy. [*sic*]

Index, 143-5 [the pages on which the index is printed]

Kant, Immanuel, *read*

Lady-bird, *see* lady-bug. Lady Bug, *meet* Lady Bird

Metamorphosis, *see* Kafka [no entry under Kafka]

Nietzsche, Friedrich, *read*

Oyster, the only mention of an, 36

Picasso, Pablo, pleasant reference to, without a trace of hostility towards, 132

Toasters, 3. If interested, *see also* bread

UCCA forms, 70. *Try* not to think about it

Warhol, Andy, inexplicable popularity of, 96, 100

Warholier-than-thou, *see* Campbell's Chicken Noodle Soup

Washing-machine, *forget it*

J.L.B.

: 14 :
Narrative by index

The final item in J. G. Ballard's volume of short stories, *War Fever* (Collins, 1990), is entitled 'The Index' – but is in fact not the book's index, but another story in index form.

According to a page-long pretended 'Editor's note', 'the text printed below is the index to the unpublished and perhaps suppressed autobiography of ... Henry Rhodes Hamilton'. It further speculates:

> Is the suppressed autobiography itself a disguised *roman à clef*, in which the fictional hero exposes the secret identities of his historical contemporaries? ... Perhaps the entire compilation is nothing more than a figment of the over-wrought imagination of some deranged lexicographer.

We can best convey the flavour and fun of this (five-page) 'index' by quoting entries from it, inviting readers to supply their own texts. (Some page references are omitted.)

> Chiang Kai-shek ... implements land-reform proposals by HRH; employs HRH as intermediary with Chou En-Lai
> Churchill, Winston ... spinal tap performed by HRH ... attacks HRH in Commons debate
> Darwin, Charles ... repudiated by HRH
> Einstein, Albert ... deathbed confession to HRH
> Eliot, T. S. ... suppresses dedication of *Four Quartets* to HRH
> Freud, Sigmund ... admits despair to HRH
> Nobel Prize, HRH nominated for, 220, 267, 342, 375, 459, 611
> Paul VI, Pope ... deplores messianic pretensions of HRH; excommunicates HRH

Yet entries without subheadings, and with abundance of page-references, may prove even more intriguing:

> Anaxagoras, 35, 67, 69-78, 481
> Byron, Lord, 28, 76, 98, 543
> Dietrich, Marlene, 234, 371, 435
> Garbo, Greta, 381
> Hadrian IV, Pope, 28, 57, 84, 119, 345-76, 411, 598
> Hayworth, Rita, 311
> Lancaster, Mrs Burt, 411

Towards the end of the index, entries suggest the ultimate fate of the author and account for the provenance of the missing text:

And this most suggestive of indexes concludes with a fitting flourish:

A good index can be much more than a guide to the contents of a book. It can often give a far clearer glimpse of its spirit than the blurb-writers or critics are able to do.

Rt Hon. Harold Macmillan,
Foreword to Indexing, the Art of, by G. Norman Knight (1977)

: III :

INDEXERS IN FICTION

What of indexers themselves? One wrote, ruefully:

'It has been suggested that there is a common indexerly nature; indeed that indexers may be fixated at one of the less attractive of Freud's psychosexual stages: that we see disorder as a sort of obscenity, that we censoriously deny the natural overflowing abundance of life and grasp at logical hierarchies as a way of reducing the boundless universe to something that will fit the mean smallness of our timid mentalities.'[1] A woman in Kurt Vonnegut's novel, *Cat's Cradle*, claims to read character from an index: 'Never index your own book,' she warns. 'It's a shameless exhibition – to the *trained* eye.'

Bernard Levin sympathetically and appreciatively saw indexers as 'shamefully treated ... Their rates of pay are disgracefully low, considering the arduousness of the work alone, never mind the skill it needs'.[2]

How indexers are generally perceived may be gauged by their representation in fiction. Many types are to be found there, not encouraging to the professional indexer. Fiction shows indexers diffident and genteel, or devoted primarily to domesticity, in some works of lady novelists; fallen pedants, such as the drunken father of the classic butler in Parkinson's *Jeeves*. Charles Kinbote, the indexer in Vladimir Nabokov's *Pale Fire*, is also the abductor, self-appointed editor, and commentator of and on the work in question, and a megalomaniac. Overall, the attitude to indexers in fiction is distinctly patronizing. Elizabeth Jane Howard's fictional author in *The Long View* (1956) describes the task, as he entrusts it doubtfully to his daughter, as 'nothing difficult. It is entirely a question of patience and concentration'. Candida Crewe's freelance indexer, Liza, in *Mad About Bees* (1991) is shown 'working away in that scatty style she found so winning'. Barbara Pym makes frequent reference to 'a thankless task' allotted to authors' wives or female friends. Angela Thirkell's aristocratic indexer displays merely amiable incompetence. Indexers in detective fiction are designated as: 'a strange sort of chap. Fussy. Methodical'; 'a meek man who drinks when he can get his hands on it'; 'the man was not responsible in the higher sense'. [3] Altogether more flattering is the description in the BBC's television drama series, 'Accident' (by Ray Jenkins, transmitted in 1979), in which a university tutor suggests indexing to a graduate student, explaining, 'It's a job that demands enormous powers of concentration and a superhuman ability to discard the irrelevant. Wonderful training for the mind.' True, true, cries the real-life indexer. Also with more proper appreciation, Judy Batchelor wrote of the hero of Penelope Lively's novel, *According to Mark* (Heinemann, 1984): 'Here surely is the indexerly mind floating free, creative, full of possibilities: the world its book, world and mind alike to be enlarged, and simultaneously diminished, by the delicate momentary attachment of a network of cognitive relationships.' [4]

Unexpected uses may be made of indexes in novels. In P. D. James's *A Mind to Murder* the medical clinic's diagnostic index serves as 'a neatly contrived apparatus for the pre-selection of a [blackmail] victim' – shocking suggestion!

Information retrieval being the chief purpose of indexing, such systems naturally figure in much detective fiction, as crime-solvers seek facts through various schemes. 'It is hardly surprising that those who devise sealed-room mysteries and Means-Motive-Opportunity charts are often aware of that perfect analytic/synthetic gadget: the card-index, and its offshoots'. [5]

1 Batchelor, Judy. Not-quite-indexers in fiction (and non-fiction). *The Indexer* 14 (4) Oct. 1985, pp 277-78
2 Bernard Levin, 'A haunting, I promise, for those who refuse to tell who's who and what's what'. *The Times*, 17 December 1976
3 Batchelor, Judy. Deer-stalkers and data banks. *The Indexer* 14 (2) Oct. 1984, pp 121-22
4 Batchelor, Judy. Not-quite-indexers in fiction.
5 Batchelor, Judy. Deer-stalkers and data banks.

Official strictures

The fictitious indexer in Anthony Trollope's *The Small House at Allington*, first published in 1862, figures as altogether the complete Civil Servant.

> The door of the big room was opened, and Mr Kissing shuffled in with very quick little steps. He shuffled in and coming direct up to John's desk, flopped his ledger down upon it. ... 'I have been half the morning, Mr Eames, looking for this letter to the Admiralty, and you've put it under S!' A bystander listening to Mr Kissing's tone would have been led to believe that the whole Income-tax Office was jeopardised by the terrible iniquity thus disclosed.
>
> 'Somerset House,' pleaded Johnny.
>
> 'Psha; – Somerset House! Half the offices in London –'
>
> 'You'd better ask Mr Love,' said Eames. 'It's all done under his special instructions.' Mr Kissing looked at Mr Love, and Mr Love looked steadfastly at his desk. 'Mr Love knows all about the indexing,' continued Johnny. 'He's index master general to the department.'
>
> 'No, I'm not, Mr Eames,' said Mr Love, who rather liked John Eames, and hated Mr Kissing with his whole heart. 'But I believe the indexes, on the whole, are very well done in this room. Some people don't know how to find letters.'
>
> 'Mr Eames,' began Mr Kissing, still pointing with a finger of bitter reproach to the misused S, and beginning an oration which was intended for the benefit of the whole room, and for the annihilation of old Mr Love, 'if you have yet to learn that the word Admiralty begins with A and not with S, you have much to learn which should have been acquired before you first came into this office. Somerset House is not a department.'

: 2 :

Indexer brought down by alcoholism

A sorry tale indeed of an indexer is found in 'The Spotted Dog' in Anthony Trollope's volume of short stories, *An Editor's Tales*; first published in *St Paul's Magazine*, then in book form in 1870.

The narrator in all the stories is a magazine editor. 'We' is editorial rather than plural. 'The Spotted Dog' opens with a letter he receives, imploring literary employment. The writer, Julius Mackenzie, gives his full life story. He is a scholar, a poet, multilingual, now living in poverty with a wife – 'not a lady' – and four children. He is 'employed on the staff of two or three of the "Penny Dreadfuls" ... I write for them matter, which we among ourselves call "blood and nastiness".'

The narrator continues:

> It so happened that at that time we had been asked to provide an index to a certain learned manuscript in three volumes. The intended publisher of the work had already procured an index from a professional compiler of such matters; but the thing had been so badly done that it could not be used. Some knowledge of the classics was required ... the gentleman who had had the task in hand had failed conspicuously, and I had been told by my enterprising friend Mr X—, the publisher, that £25 would be freely paid on the proper accomplishment of the undertaking. The work, apparently so trifling in its nature, demanded a scholar's acquirements, and could hardly be completed in less than two months. We had snubbed the offer, saying that we should be ashamed to ask an educated man to give his time and labour for so small a remuneration; – but to Mr Julius Mackenzie £25 for two months' work would manifestly be a godsend.

Mackenzie comes for interview and is obviously a drunkard. Asked to give a reference, '"Mr Grimes of the Spotted Dog knows me better than anyone else" said he'. The editor duly visits the pub, where the landlord's wife, Mrs Grimes, assures him, 'As for book learning, sir; – it doesn't matter what language it is, it's all as one to him. He knows 'em all round ... he knows off by heart whole books full of learning.' However, she also tells Mackenzie, 'He's got a bad wife, sir; the worst as ever was. Talk of drink – there's nothing that woman wouldn't do for it.'

The Doctor, the author of the work, 'was charmed with our account of the man, and saw with his mind's eye the work, for the performance of which he was pining, perfected in a manner that would be a blessing to the scholars of all future ages'. ... The editor engages him:

The manuscript was produced upon the table. If he would undertake the work and perform it, he should be paid £8:6s:8d for each of the three volumes as they were completed. ... At first he was in ecstasies, and as we explained to him the way in which the index should be brought out and the codification performed, he turned over the pages rapidly, and showed us that he understood at any rate the nature of the work to be done. But when we came to details he was less happy.

He wants to work on the index in the pub. The narrator visits Mrs Grimes again to arrange a room there for him to work in.

The prospective indexer meets the author:

The volumes of the ms were displayed upon the table. The compiler of them, as he lifted here a page and there a page, handled them with the gentleness of a lover. They had been exquisitely arranged, and were very fair. The pagings, and the margins, and the chapterings, and all the complementary paraphernalia of authorship, were perfect. ... When it was suggested that references would be required, it seemed that [Mackenzie] did know his way into the library of the British Museum.

Before the end of the first month the index of the first volume, nearly completed, had been sent down for the inspection of the Doctor [the author], and had been returned with ample eulogium and some little criticism. The criticisms Mackenzie answered by letter, with true scholarly spirit, and the Doctor was delighted. ... When he found that the work was really in industrious hands, he ceased to be clamorous for early publication ... Mackenzie had certainly found a most efficient friend in the author whose works had been confided to his hands.

Ultimately, though, drunkenness and despair prevail. Mackenzie threatens suicide; the editor suggests Mackenzie comes for a walk with him, and has first to put away the papers in the pub bedroom, with Mrs Grimes's assistance.

We were astonished to find how much she had come to know about the work. Added to the Doctor's manuscript there were now the pages of Mackenzie's indexes,—and there were other pages of references, for use in making future indexes, – as to all of which Mrs Grimes seemed to be quite at home.

Alas, Mackenzie's wife burns the ms, and he cuts his throat.

Indexing in Baker Street

We know that Sherlock Holmes did not wish to learn or remember anything that would not be useful to him in his work as a consulting detective.[1] We also know that he was a mine of information on criminal cases of all kinds, and could almost always produce a former example of the circumstances before him, however bizarre. He could recall cases at will, and quote them offhand, but he did not rely only on memory; he had a reference library and a filing system. Dr. Watson tells us of a 'line of reference books beside the mantelpiece', from which Holmes 'picked a red-covered volume' to read about 'Robert Walsingham de Vere St. Simon, second son of the Duke of Balmoral'.[2] This volume must have been Burke's Peerage, and other books on Holmes's reference shelf – 'books which anyone may be supposed to possess' – were Bradshaw (the vocabulary of which Holmes memorably pronounced to be 'nervous and terse, but limited'), and *Whitaker's Almanack*.[3] But Watson was obviously not index-minded, and his mentions of Holmes's records are tantalisingly vague and unhelpful.

However, let us assemble what material there is about Holmes as an indexer:

> One winter's night, as we sat together by the fire, I ventured to suggest to him that, as he had finished pasting extracts into his commonplace book, he might employ the next two hours in making our room more habitable.[4]
>
> He took down the great book in which, day by day, he filed the agony columns of the various London journals.

The first quotation suggests only one book for cuttings; the second suggests a special book for agony columns. But Watson is well known to have been rather careless about details, and earlier in his association with Holmes (1889), he observed that there were several books, which agrees better with other statements:

> Then Sherlock Holmes pulled down from the shelf one of the ponderous volumes in which he pasted his cuttings. "Here is an advertisement which will interest you", said he. "It appeared in all the papers

about a year ago. Listen to this: 'Lost on the 9th inst., Mr. Jeremiah Hayling, aged 20, a hydraulic engineer . . .'[6]

It seems, then, that Holmes kept all newspaper cuttings of interest to him, and that 'day by day' he pasted them into large books. He also indexed them: 'So spake Sherlock Holmes, and turned back to the great scrap book in which he was arranging and indexing some of his recent material.'[7]

Note that he was 'arranging and indexing' in the same scrap book. We can perhaps conclude from the next quotation that Holmes sorted his material alphabetically into separate volumes for each letter, pasted the items into the volumes as they came to hand, and made indexes at the ends of the volumes.

> 'Make a long arm, Watson, and see what V has to say'. I leaned back and took down the great index volume to which he referred. Holmes balanced it on his knee, and his eyes moved slowly and lovingly over the record of old cases, mixed with the accumulated information of a life-time. 'Voyage of the *Gloria Scott*', he read . . . 'Victor Lynch, the forger. Venomous lizard or glia ... Vittoria, the circus belle. Vanderbilt and the Yeggman . . . Vipers. Vigor, the Hammersmith wonder. Hullo! Hullo! Good old index. You can't beat it. Listen to this, Watson. Vampirism in Hungary. And again, Vampires in Transylvania'. He turned over the pages with eagerness, but after a short intent perusal he threw down the great book with a snarl of disappointment.[8]

Here we note that both Holmes and Watson called these giant volumes indexes, but the term was used loosely, since the actual records were present. The non-alphabetical arrangement of the items in this V volume is apparent, as Holmes recites the subjects on the pages he is turning over. He is not in a hurry, and prefers to browse among his cuttings, rather than to locate Vampires directly by means of the index pages. It is a little surprising to find Victor Lynch the forger here instead of in the L volume, and Voyage of the *Gloria Scott*, rather than *Gloria Scott*, Voyage of the, under G, but Holmes was always idiosyncratic. Venomous lizard was perhaps put under V rather than L to associate it with other venomous creatures, such as swamp adders,[9] and *Cyanea capillata.*[10]

The division of the news cuttings into a volume for each letter is confirmed by another account: 'Holmes shot out a long arm and picked out volume H of his encyclopaedia of reference.'[11] This passage goes on to give details in peerage fashion of the Duke of Holderness. It seems unlikely that an actual encyclopaedia can be meant;

encyclopaedias seldom deal with contemporary peers, nor do their volumes usually cover a single letter of the alphabet. We must assume that Watson is again referring to a volume of Holmes's own compiling.

There is one more item, showing another stage in Holmes's information retrieval system: 'Holmes sat moodily at one side of the fire, cross-indexing his records of crime.'[12] This, we imagine, involved relating one volume to another, for example directing a search for the *Gloria Scott* from Volume G to Volume V, where the details were to be found.

There are other references to Sherlock Holmes' Criminal Index to be found in 'A Scandal in Bohemia':

> "The facts are briefly these: Some five years ago, during a lengthy visit to Warsaw, I made the acquaintance of the well-known adventuress, Irene Adler. The name is no doubt familiar to you."
>
> "Kindly look her up in my index, Doctor," murmured Holmes without opening his eyes. For many years he had adopted a system of docketing all paragraphs concerning men and things, so that it was difficult to name a subject or a person on which he could not at once furnish information. In this case I found her biography sandwiched in between that of a Hebrew rabbi and that of a staff-commander who had written a monograph upon the deep-sea fishes.
>
> "Let me see!" said Holmes. "Hum! Born in New Jersey in the year 1858. Contralto—hum! La Scala, hum! Prima donna Imperial Opera of Warsaw—yes! Retired from operatic stage—ha! Living in London—quite so! Your Majesty, as I understand, became entangled with this young person, wrote her some compromising letters, and is now desirous of getting those letters back."

In 'A Case of Identity':

> "Quite an interesting study, that maiden," he observed. "I found her more interesting than her little problem, which, by the way, is rather a trite one. You will find parallel cases, if you consult my index, in Andover in '77, and there was something of the sort at The Hague last year. Old as is the idea, however, there were one or two details which were new to me."

and in 'The Adventure of the Empty House':

> "Just give me down my index of biographies from the shelf."
>
> He turned over the pages lazily, leaning back in his chair and blowing great clouds from his cigar.
>
> "My collection of M's is a fine one," said he. "Moriarty himself is enough to make any letter illustrious, and here is Morgan the poisoner, and Merridew of abominable memory, and Mathews, who

knocked out my left canine in the waiting-room at Charing Cross, and, finally, here is our friend of to-night."

He handed over the book, and I read:

'Moran, Sebastian, Colonel. Unemployed. Formerly 1st Bangalore Pioneers. Born London, 1840. Son of Sir Augustus Moran, C. B., once British Minister to Persia. Educated Eton and Oxford. Served in Jowaki Campaign, Afghan Campaign, Charasiab (despatches), Sherpur, and Cabul. Author of Heavy Game of the Western Himalayas (1881); Three Months in the Jungle (1884). Address: Conduit Street. Clubs: The Anglo-Indian, the Tankerville, the Bagatelle Card Club.

On the margin was written, in Holmes's precise hand: "The second most dangerous man in London."

We can conclude that Holmes was a successful indexer. He was industrious and painstaking, as all indexers must be, and, aided by his remarkable memory, his filing system never failed him. A modern practitioner would no doubt have made a master card-index for all the encyclopaedic volumes, but Holmes did very well without.

M.D.A.

Did any of my readers ever busy him- or herself with index-making? There requires one or two pressures to persevere in it: enthusiasm of a high order, which is unflagging, or the necessity of earning daily bread.

William Kingsford, *Canadian Archaeology* (1886)

References

1 A Study in Scarlet	2 The Noble Bachelor	3 The Valley of Fear
4 The Musgrave Ritual	5 The Red Circle	6 The Engineer's Thumb
7 The Red Circle	8 The Sussex Vampires	9 The Speckled Band
10 The Lion's Mane	11 The Priory School	12 The Five Orange Pips

All by Arthur Conan Doyle

Absorption and love

The first indexer presented to us by Angela Thirkell appears in her novel, *Northbridge Rectory* (Hamish Hamilton, 1941):

> Having shut the door behind his Egeria, [Mr Downing] went back to his work and was soon so absorbed in making his index, for he prided himself on his very complete indexing with every possible cross-reference, flattering allusions to which were frequently made in reviews, that time slipped by unheeded.

While in Thirkell's *County Chronicle* (Hamish Hamilton, 1950):

> "And while I was in Barchester", says Lord Silverbridge, "I bought a card index. You know, a kind of whatnot with very long drawers and you put A to C and X to Z on them and write things on cards and then don't know where you've put them."

He goes on to explain that though he works for a publisher, 'turning a fairly honest penny', all the card index stuff is done by a secretary. 'The other day she was out and I wasted hours looking for one of our authors called Spenderton-Cook because she had put him under E.'

Isabel Dale, the heroine, whom he's just met, falls for this and says she supposes it was a mistake. 'As a matter of fact it wasn't,' says Lord Silverbridge, 'at least not exactly. His name is Evan-Spenderton-Cook and sometimes he hyphens them all and sometimes he doesn't. But I thought the secretary could have done a kind of cross-indexing if that's the right word and put them in under everything. She's one of those educated young women that are obviously going to bully their employers all their lives till they marry one of them.'

Actually this is just ill will, for we do not find him henpecked at all, by anyone, not even the ebullient Lady Cora, his sister. Nor is this gifted pianist quite so dumb on indexing as he appears, and when Isabel and he and the card index cabinet are sitting together, at this juncture with a chaperon and a teatray, he soon gets the hang of it. Why is Isabel the expert? Well, she is a leading light in the Barchester Hospital Libraries, like some others of Angela

Thirkell's heroines, and, unknown to his Lordship, is author of some of his favourite books, which she writes anagrammatically under the name of Lisa Bedale. She is also a natural genius with everybody's papers.

You may want to know why the Duke of Omnium's heir is messing about with his own card index at all. This is quickly answered. Unlike Isabel's other potential suitor who is absorbed with a newly-discovered variant on Bohun's 'Sonnet on his Mistress's Pox', Silverbridge has a real book in hand, the *War History of the Barsetshire Yeomanry*. By page 292 of *County Chronicle* he has mastered the card index, and although its use is never quite explained to us, one gathers it enables him to find details of the members of the Yeomanry. By this time Isabel is helping him to sort out the reminiscent contributions and the work is likely to be completed within a year. However, Mrs Thirkell's novel itself has to finish quite soon – it has only 348 pages – and when the Conservative 'do' is over Silverbridge proposes to Isabel and is accepted. Their union is going to be most useful to the Omniums: Isabel has just become heiress to what sounds like millions, and the Omniums are a bit strapped for cash. Silverbridge is now going to be able to stand for Parliament – guess in whose interest? I hope he doesn't lose sight of the card index, which has done much for him and must be one of the most important indexes in English fiction, at least to the followers of Barsetshire fortunes.

J.D.L.

Any simpleton may write a book, but it requires high skill to make an index.

Rossiter Johnson (1840-1931)

Deer-stalkers and data banks

It is hardly surprising that those who devise sealed-room mysteries and Means-Motive-Opportunity charts are often aware of that perfect analytic/synthetic gadget: the card-index, and its offshoots. Indexes and catalogues play their part in the detection process. The hero of Jocelyn Davey's *A Touch of Stage Fright* (Chatto and Windus, 1960) seeks clues in the minor writings of a critic called Forsyte: 'The library's indexing proved fabulous – a match for the peculiar hide-and-seek game that Forsyte had apparently played in his later years among America's innumerable "little magazines".'

A lady answers a telephone enquiry in Lawrence Block's *The Burglar in the Closet* (Pocket Books, New York, 1978):

> '... you can try Gag. That's initials, G-A-G, it's Gotham Artists' Guild. They're a reference service, you go there and they have slides of everybody's work in their files, plus they have everything indexed by artists' names, and they can tell you what gallery handles an artist's work or how to get in touch with him directly if he doesn't have any gallery affiliation. They're located somewhere in midtown, I think in the East Fifties. Gotham Artists' Guild.'

To which the enquirer, though he has never met the lady, very properly replies, 'I think I love you'.

Dead for a Penny by Charles A. Goodrum (Gollancz, 1979) allows us to share in engrossing detail the hunt, in ever-decreasing circles, through a vast data bank for the vital factor linking a series of coin-thefts. Just as the librarian who is guiding the detectives in their quest (George thought, 'Thank God there are librarians; this young lady could only be a librarian or a nun') is about to bring on screen the final and decisive information, 'the computer streamed a paragraph across the center of the screen: "The Capital Line program will be inoperative for approximately four hours for maintenance and update". "****!" said the virginal Miss Arnette.'

Indexing is much discussed, with knowledge and passion, by some characters in *Dead for a Penny*:

'Those of us on the research side [are] in love with knowledge, any knowledge, and to us the end is to gather it in and store it and then get it back when we need it ... We've gone from lists to indexes to bibliographies to catalogs to the computer! We've got the stuff into digital form and can cut back and forth by Boolean logic till hell won't have it. The Millennium at last! ... We always treated our great card catalogs as a sort of joke. We all took them for granted and we let them die ...'

But computer-error is not an occasional anomaly; it is all-pervasive. When a great Library in this novel did a test-run almost ten thousand entries were erased through a programming error. 'They think they were able to reconstruct it ... that many books, that many documents, that much of our written experience is taken from us. We're blinded ...' although, as this speaker thinks to himself later: '... the worst question is, Should we even be concerned at the loss of bits of data? Might not forgetting clear the way to new thoughts and new solutions?' The author is however aware that the need for economy and efficiency may make a manual subject index fallible in a different way. His librarian explains: 'You have to out-guess us librarians, or the book is completely lost to you. You always have to go up the vocabulary from the very specific to the general. We stop with the bottom rung ... [card catalogs] look so organized, they intimidate the user. "They must know what they're doing—I must be doing it wrong"'.

In Michael Gilbert's *Smallbone Deceased* (Hodder and Stoughton, 1950), the Horniman Alphabetical Index used by the solicitors Horniman, Birley & Crane has almost the personality of a character in the novel. Every letter sent from the office is numbered, filed, indexed in impeccable detail and eventually, if it pertains to a 'first-class' client, lodged in 'a Horniman dust-proof, moisture-proof, air-proof and indeed mouse-proof Box'. When the corpse of one Marcus Smallbone is found in the deed-box bearing his own name, it is the omission of all these meticulous preliminary procedures that provides the mystery, and therefore the plot, of the book. Clearly the murderer had none of an indexer's instincts.

In P. D. James's *A Mind to Murder* (Faber, 1963) indexers may grieve to see to what evil uses their professional labours may be put. Having learned that detailed information regarding patients, including 'sexual aberration, kleptomania, or any other socially unacceptable personality disorder', is coded on to punched cards in the medical director's diagnostic index, retrievable by selected combinations of codes, Superintendent Dalgliesh declares it 'A neatly contrived apparatus for the pre-selection of a Blackmail victim'. However, he concedes, 'no system is completely proof against clever and deliberate wickedness'.

When indexers appear as characters in these books, less than decent respect for the profession is often shown. An early P. D. James, *Unnatural Causes* (Faber, 1967), has one of the characters describe the murdered man, an author: 'He must have been a strange sort of chap. Fussy. Methodical. That card index, for instance.' The wretched Mantel, in *No Better Fiend* by Edmund McGirr (Gollancz, 1971) (which also has some divertingly drawn encyclopaedists and publishers among its characters), seems to have lived in a penurious half-world of near-Dickensian squalor, hovering between peccadillo and crime: the encyclopaedia-editor Boat, who has commissioned indexing work from Mantel in the past but recently told him, after an ethical lapse, that he would not require his services again, says of him, 'Poverty and his vices drove him to a despicable action, but the man was not responsible in the higher sense'.

In *The Weight of the Evidence* by Michael Innes (Gollancz, 1944, Chapter XIII), an Inspector investigating a murder officially visits a Professor, and finds him 'peacefully arranging multi-coloured slips of pasteboard in a card index'. The Inspector feels 'that he was at last gaining a convincing breath of that higher and rarefied air which academic persons are supposed wontedly to breathe.'

This indexer, in fact, has inadvertently killed a colleague, and is hastening to complete his work before the retribution he knows must fall – a deadly deadline indeed..

K. Giles in *Death in Diamonds* (Gollancz, 1967) refers disparagingly to: 'A meek man who drinks when he can get his hands on it ... He indexes learned tomes'. Well, really; try transposing those two main verbs, K. Giles, and you may be nearer the mark.

J.L.B.

: 6 :

Ladies at work

Barbara Pym may be regarded as the patron novelist of indexers. Not only do several indexers appear among her cast of characters, but characters from one story may make some appearances in subsequent novels, forming a network of allusions, addenda and cross-references in true indexerly style. Pym was herself for over 25 years in charge of publications of the International African Institute, and compiled the indexes; work that she greatly enjoyed. Her two indexer-heroines are those who most resemble their author, as her friend and colleague Hazel Holt has averred.

Pym's indexers make their first appearance in her second novel, *Excellent Women* (Cape, 1952). Foremost among them is Esther Clovis, secretary of a Learned (anthropological) Society; a formidable and recurring figure, seen by the narrator, Mildred Lathbury, as having 'hair like a dog, but a very capable person, respected and esteemed by Everard Bone, and, moreover, one who could make an index and correct proofs'.

Less impressively, the wife of the President of the Learned Society always attends its meetings, knits, and drops off to sleep. Mildred asks Everard:

'Did she work with him in the field?'
'Good Heavens, no! She knows nothing at all about anthropology.'
'Didn't she even do the index or proofreading for one of his books? You know what it often says in a preface or dedication—"To my wife, who undertook the arduous duty of proof-reading" or making the index.'
'She may have done that. After all, it's what wives are for.'

After that, we should not be surprised by the following dialogue, when Mildred is invited to dinner by Everard, an anthropologist. She asks how his book is progressing:

'I have just had some of the proofs and then of course the index will have to be done. I don't know how I'm going to find time to do it,' said Everard.
'But aren't there people who do things like that?' I asked.
'You mean excellent women whom one respects and esteems? ...

I was wondering ... but no – I couldn't ask you. You're much too busy, I'm sure.'

'But I don't know how to do these things,' I protested.

'Oh, but I could show you,' he said eagerly; 'you'd soon learn.' He got up and fetched a bundle of proof sheets and typescript from the desk. 'It's quite simple, really. All you have to do is see that the proof agrees with the typescript.'

'Well, I dare say I could do that,' I said, taking a sheet of proof and looking at it doubtfully.

'Oh, splendid. How very good of you!'

I had never seen Everard so enthusiastic before. 'And perhaps you could help me with the index too? Reading proofs for a long stretch gets a little boring. The index would make a nice change for you.'

'Yes, it would make a nice change,' I agreed. And before long I should be certain to find myself at his sink peeling potatoes and washing up; that would be a nice change when both proof-reading and indexing began to pall. Was any man worth this burden? Probably not, but one shouldered it bravely and cheerfully ...

'It should be interesting work,' I said rather formally and began to read from the proof sheet I was holding. But as I read a feeling of despair came over me, for it was totally incomprehensible. 'But I don't understand it!' I cried out. 'How can I ever know what it really means?'

'Oh, never mind about that,' said Everard, smiling. 'I dare say you will eventually.'

In Pym's next novel, *Jane and Prudence* (Cape, 1953), we find Miss Clothier, who works in a 'vague cultural organization' where she 'drew a small card index towards her and began moving the cards here and there with her fingers, as if she were coaxing music from some delicate instrument'. Pym's etheral appreciation of card indexes is shown again in *An Unsuitable Attachment* (Macmillan 1982), where this dialogue occurs:

> 'One feels that anything to do with card indexes is more in a woman's line.'
>
> 'You mean it's slightly degrading?'
>
> 'Oh, no. A card index may be a noble thing.'

Pym's sixth novel, *No Fond Return of Love* (Cape, 1961), intertwines indexing and romance. The cover of Granada's paperback edition of 1981 displays a sheaf of index cards, the first inscribed '*Love in the Western World* (Rougemont)', with a heart cut out, floating away. It opens with the splendid affirmation: 'There are various ways of mending a broken heart, but perhaps going to a learned conference is one of the more unusual.'

There, the heroine, Dulcie, who 'did most of her work at home ... and had built up a useful reputation as a competent indexer and proof-corrector', finds that her fellow conference members 'all correct proofs, make bibliographies and indexes'. During the conference a lay reader 'tried to show how all work can be done to the Glory of God, even making an index'. During it also, Dulcie meets the editor with whom at last she finds true love.

The title Pym first chose for this novel, and preferred, was *No Thankless Task*. In it, Dulcie asks, 'Do we all correct proofs, make bibliographies and indexes, and do all the rather humdrum thankless tasks for people more brilliant than ourselves?' She reflects, 'A book can be made or marred by its index ... remembering the wives and others who undertook what was often acknowledged to be a thankless task'; and refers to acknowledgements:

'Something about your having undertaken the arduous or thankless – though I hope it won't be that – task of compiling the index.'

Charmingly and fittingly, Hazel Holt's biography of Barbara Pym, *A Lot to Ask* (Macmillan, 1990), includes this acknowledgement:

I would like to thank Barbara's sister Hilary Walton, without whom this book would not have been possible. She has, of course, been an invaluable source of information and has shown herself to be a true friend by undertaking the thankless task of compiling the index.

A hundred million entries

The mathematician and philosopher, Bertrand Russell, at the age of 80 turned to writing 'a series of moral satires'. He told Stanley Unwin that he had 'broken out in a new place and taken to writing *Fantastic Stories*'. Unwin published two collections of these, *Satan in the Suburbs* in 1953, and *Nightmares of Eminent Persons* in 1954.

The second volume includes 'The Theologian's Nightmare', in which a theologian dreams that he dies and arrives at the door of heaven to find that the janitor has never heard of man. The heavenly librarian is called, 'a globular being with a thousand eyes', who knows nothing of Earth, the Solar System or the Milky Way, but thinks he has 'heard the word "galaxy" before. In fact, I believe that one of our sub-librarians specialises in galaxies'.

The galactic sub-librarian, 'a dodecahedron. It was clear that at one time his surface had been bright, but the dust of the shelves had rendered him dim and opaque', explains that there are a hundred million galaxies, and each has a volume to itself. He sets off to find information about the Milky Way.

"Some three weeks later, he returned, explaining that the extraordinarily efficient card-index in the galactic section of the library had enabled them to locate the galaxy. 'We have employed,' he said, 'all the five thousand clerks in the galactic section on this search'."

The theologian demands a closer search, specifying the Solar System and the Sun as objects. The sub-librarian tells him, 'I believe that at one time a list of the whole three hundred billion stars was demanded by the Administration and that it is still stored in the basement. I will engage special labour from the Other Place to search for this particular star'.

It is several years before 'a very weary and dispirited tetrahedron' reports that he has 'discovered the particular star concerning which inquiries have been made'.

: 8 :

A shameless exhibition

A chapter of Kurt Vonnegut's *Cat's Cradle* (Michael Joseph, 1963) bears the admonitory title, 'Never index your own book'. The narrator has read an autobiography written by a friend of his, and is admiring the index.

As for the life of Aamons, Mona, the index itself gave a jangling, surrealistic picture of the many conflicting forces that had been brought to bear on her and of her dismayed reactions to them.

'Aamons, Mona', the index said, 'adopted by Monzano in order to boost Monzano's popularity, 194-199, 216n; childhood in compound of House of Hope and Mercy, 63-81; childhood romance with P. Castle, 72f., death of father, 89ff; death of mother, 92f; embarrassed by role as national erotic symbol, 80, 95, 166n., 209, 247n., 400-406, 566n., 678, engaged to P. Castle, 193; essential naiveté, 67-71, 80, 95f, 116n., 209, 274n., 400-406, 566n., 678; lives with Bokonon, 92-98, 196-197; poems about, 2n., 26, 114, 119, 311, 316, 477n., 501, 507, 555n., 689, 718ff, 799ff, 800n., 841, 846ff, 908n., 971, 974; poems by, 89, 92, 193; returns to Monzano, 199; returns to Bokonon, 197; runs away from Bokonon, 199; runs away from Monzano, 197; tries to make self ugly in order to stop being erotic symbol to islanders, 80, 95f, 116n., 209, 247n., 400-406, 566n., 678; tutored by Bokonon, 63-80; writes letter to United Nations, 200; xylophone virtuoso, 71.'

I showed this index entry to the Mintons, asking them if they didn't think it was an enchanting biography in itself, a biography of a reluctant goddess of love. I got an unexpectedly expert answer, as one does in life sometimes; it appeared that Claire Minton, in her time, had been a professional indexer. I had never heard of such a professional before.

She told me she had put her husband through college years before with her earnings as an indexer, that the earnings had been good, and that few people could index well.

She said that indexing was a thing that only the most amateurish author undertook to do for his own book. I asked her what she thought of Philip Castle's job.

'Flattering to the author, insulting to the reader,' she said. 'In a hyphenated word,' she observed, with the shrewd amiability of an expert, "self-indulgent". I'm always embarrassed when I see an index an author has made of his own work.'

'Embarrassed?'

'It's a revealing thing, an author's index of his own work,' she informed me. 'It's a shameless exhibition – to the trained eye.'

'She can read character from an index,' said her husband.

'Oh?' I said. 'What can you tell about Philip Castle?' She smiled faintly. 'Things I'd better not tell strangers.'

'Sorry.'

'He's obviously in love with this Mona Aamons Monzano,' she said. ... 'He has mixed feelings about his father.'

'That's true of every man on earth.' I egged her on gently.

'He's insecure.'

'What mortal isn't?' I demanded.

'He'll never marry her.'

'Why not?'

'I've said all I'm going to say,' she said.

'I'm gratified to meet an indexer who respects the privacy of others.'

'Never index your own book,' she stated.

A duprass, Bokonon tells us, is a valuable instrument for gaining and developing, in the privacy of an interminable love affair, insights that are queer but true. The Mintons' cunning exploration of indexes was surely a case in point. A duprass, Bokonon tells us, is also a sweetly conceited establishment. The Mintons' establishment was no exception.

Some time later, Ambassador Minton and I met in the aisle of the airplane, away from his wife, and he showed that it was important to him that I respect what his wife could find out from indexes.

'You know why Castle will never marry the girl, even though he loves her, even though she loves him, even though they grew up together?' he whispered.

'No, sir, I don't.'

'Because he's a homosexual,' whispered Minton. 'She can tell that from an index, too.'

: 9 :

If unpublished, burn

Georges Perec, who gives us something of just about everything, has also given us in *Life: a User's Manual: Fictions* (first published in French, 1970; see above page 119), an indexer of sorts. This is one Monsieur Jérôme, who is being paid 'one hundred and fifty francs a month to make a card index of the Spanish clergy. In five years he had made out seven thousand four hundred and sixty-two biographies of churchmen in office in the reigns of Philip III (1598-1621), Philip IV (1621-1625) and Charles II (1665-1700), and had sorted them under twenty-seven different headings...'

His patron dies; after fruitless efforts to find a publisher he 'took his manuscript ... to burn it in the courtyard of the Sorbonne, which incidentally cost him a night in a policestation.'

The full history of Monsieur Jérôme is to be found in the checklist at the end of the novel under: 'The Tale of the History Teacher who was cultural attaché in the subcontinent.'

J.L.B.

A character in Robertson Davies's novel, World of Wonders *(The Macmillan Company of Canada, 1975) tells his enemy, 'When your autobiography comes out I shall look for myself in the index under S and C: "Squirts I have known, Mungo Fetch", and "Climbers I have encountered, Fetch, M.".*

: 10 :

Infatuation with a swarming index

Homer and his wife Mary are historians, teaching at Harvard, in Jane Langton's crime fiction, *The Memorial Hall Murder* (Penguin, 1974). As academics do, they are writing a book:

> The two of them were taking turns, rewriting the lectures into chapters. Mary was way ahead of him. She had finished all her chapters. She was working on the index. She was clucking at him to hurry up.

Through a chance encounter Homer gets involved in a bit of sleuthing, but continues to make progress on the book:

> He was supposed to be finishing the last chapter of the textbook, *The Great Cloud Darkening the Land*, which was growing out of the course of lectures. But he was bored with the last chapter. It was the index that really captured his interest. The index was going to be the best part. It was going to be the most informative, garrulous, cross-indexed index there ever was. A magnificent index. At the moment the index was only a crawling swarm of three-by-five cards, proliferating all over the table. Homer put his hand into the pile at random and plucked out a single card.

The couple have some unorthodox (if companionable) working methods: after a Saturday walk, "Mary turned around to go home to work on her half of the index, with which she was as infatuated as Homer".

The mystery is solved before the book is published, and reviewed, so we cannot judge of the final quality of this so cherished index.

: II :

Eccentric, shabby, and normally drunk

The father of the perfection of butlers, from *Jeeves: a Gentleman's Personal Gentleman* by C. Northcote Parkinson (Macdonald and Jane's Publishers Ltd, 1979), is a daunting example of an indexer in fiction, thus depicted:

> The Rev. Theophilus Jeeves ... pinned all his hopes on Basil, who took no fewer than three prizes for scripture at Hogsnorton Grammar School. Nor was Theophilus initially disappointed, for young Basil went on to obtain a scholarship to Oriel College, Oxford, where he presently graduated with honours. Somewhat to his father's dismay, however, the young man declined to take holy orders and proposed rather to remain at Oxford as a lecturer in philology.

A drunken contretemps at what should have been a learned lecture to the Philological Society put a final period to what might have been a distinguished career.

> For the rest of his life Basil was to make a scanty living as a proof-reader and index- compiler. We may picture him as eccentric, shabby, learned and normally drunk. One thing he always retained, however, would seem to have been a magnificent and pedantic command of the English language. When relatively sober, at least, his periods were rounded, his syntax perfect, his vocabulary extensive and his *mots* supremely *justes* ... Reginald [Jeeves] ... owed his upbringing to his father. If Reginald went to school there is no record of it. We must rather suppose that life with Basil Jeeves, as he swayed over his proof sheets, was an education in itself.

Archives of oblivion

The narrator of Graham Swift's 'psychological thriller' *Shuttlecock* (Allen Lane, 1981; Penguin, 1982), complains, 'What blander job is there than a librarian's? And then, as with any work, ours too is routine. Most of the time is spent in mundane chores like cataloguing and indexing.'

Worse is to come: the Head of the police archives in this novel proves to be an anti-indexer, an obliterator rather than retrieval-facilitator of information. He searches his soul:

'All this information we sit on, Prentis. Do you know how I sometimes imagine this place? A big cupboard for the collected skeletons of half the metropolitan population ... Just think for a moment of all those innocent, unwitting people whose peace of mind might be shattered by some little titbit we have here ... I started to think that precisely because I had access to all this evil, I was in a position to do real good. I thought, perhaps one can wipe out certain harms simply by erasing the record of those harms.'

He proceeds to act on this principle of information obliteration:

'I believed I could get rid of knowledge on other people's behalf – before it became their knowledge ... I started to take files from the shelves ... I started to destroy information. I used to think: here is such and such an individual – just a name in a file – who will now never have to know some ruinous piece of information. He'll never even know his benefactor. I used to think I was actually ridding the world of trouble.'

: 13 :

Lively indexers

There are several characters in the novels of Penelope Lively who practise indexing and allied research. In her *Perfect Happiness* (Heinemann, 1983) there is a gratifying, Pym-like affair suggesting that, yes, indexing can indeed lead to romance. Frances and Morris meet at a party, where –

> She told him about her new house, and the job, and he told her about the progress of his book and his problems with compiling such things as bibliography and index. "I'm a mere journalist," he said. "I've never had to deal with these refinements before."
>
> "I once did an index for Steven," said Frances. "It's not so difficult. The thing is to have all these little cards . . ." Morris Corfield nodded gravely as she talked, appearing to take careful note. The conversation, it occurred to Frances, was becoming somewhat banal. She said, "All this is rather dull." Morris nodded in acquiescence and then jumped slightly.
>
> "Not at all. Absolutely not." Frances laughed. "You were getting a glazed look."
>
> "I was concentrating," he said.

Later, Morris recalls this meeting, thinking, 'She had given him some guidance about indexing, of which she apparently had experience, and he had tried to give the impression of taking note while searching for some way to ensure another meeting.'

He invites her to a dinner party, asks her to remain when the other guests leave, and:

> "Tell me about indexing," said Morris.
>
> "I told you about indexing, at Zoe's party. Didn't I?"
>
> "Yes," said Morris. "I'm afraid I didn't listen properly."
>
> Frances laughed. "You can't really want me to tell you the technicalities of indexing for the second time at ... at a quarter past midnight."

Two weeks later, on their second outing together, he tells her:

> "I've been putting into practice your advice about indexing. The thing begins to look more shapely."
>
> "Good," said Frances. And beamed. "It's nice to be useful."

At which point he takes her hand ...

A life-time's task

Lewis Percy, the eponymous (hardly) hero of Anita Brookner's novel (Cape, 1989), is, like many of her fictional characters, a librarian, academic and ineffectual. The progress of the card-index he works on through the book appears an indication of his cautious, regular, low-key attitudes to life.

On receiving his doctorate for a study of French literature, Percy starts work in the university library,

> cataloguing articles in the many publications allotted to him. This subject index kept him in touch with work in his field and even with work outside it. It was not uninteresting; it had a certain dignity. He was aware that he needed a dignity of his own, and was glad to find it in his work.

In his greatest humiliation, when his wife has left him, Percy seeks refuge in his index: 'He looked humbly round him at the library, and applied himself with infinite care to his index cards.' When a new career lecturing in America is in prospect, the 'beguiling normality' of the index nearly conquers:

> Lewis found it so soothing that he almost abandoned thoughts of departure and a new life. Like a man in a trance he raised his eyes every few minutes to the clock: every catalogue card took on the lustre of a reliquary.

The index is on-going, requiring constant updating ('You're supposed to be doing that for the rest of your life,' his friend tells him) – and hand-written. When Percy proposes that it should be typed, and on larger cards, his shocked superior declares himself unable to take the responsibility of authorizing such a rash departure from settled ways.

Then comes the new technology, though, fervently welcomed by the Chief Librarian, who exults in the prospect of new sources of funding, extra staff, training sessions, altogether new systems, a younger clientele. He heralds the new era to his indexer:

> 'You won't have to do that much longer, Lewis,' said Goldsborough. 'Once we've installed the computers,' he added ...

'Just as a matter of interest, Arnold, what will happen to the index?'

'But my dear fellow!' exclaimed Goldsborough. 'This will be the index's finest hour! The index will henceforth be immortal. The index, Lewis, will be transformed into a permanent record. By you,' he added.

'You mean,' said Lewis slowly, 'that I transfer the index? That I key it in, or whatever one does, right from the beginning? In other words, that I start doing it all over again? This will create years of backlog, Arnold.'

But Lewis escapes this labour, fleeing to a new career in a new country with a new woman; so we never learn whether he would have come to approve and appreciate the machinery.

A good index has the satisfying qualities of all skilled workmanship; an inspired index may be a thing of joy – sometimes wittier, more eloquent and more enlightening than the book whose train it follows with such deceptive humility.

Kevin Jackson, *Invisible Forms* (1999)

Lady obstructionist

There are many scholars and researchers of different types in A.S. Byatt's extraordinarily complex novel about biographical research, *Possession* (Chatto & Windus, 1990), so we need not feel too despondent that the most demonstrably indexing one among them is Beatrice Nest – a plump lady don nearing retirement, seen as an 'obstructive white sheep'. Readers find her ensconced in her 'small cavern constructed of filing cabinets', meeting a request from a colleague for access to the vast 19th-century journal she has worked on for more than twenty years.

'Is there any way of checking?'
'I could look at my card index.'
'Could I see your card index, Beatrice?'
'Oh, I don't know, it's all a bit of a muddle, I have my own system, you know, Roland, for recording things, I think I'd better look myself, I can better understand my own hieroglyphics.'
... She began to move things across her desk, a heavy wooden-handled knitting bag, several greying parcels of unopened books. There was a whole barbican of index boxes, thick with dust and scuffed with age, which she ruffled in interminably, talking to herself.
'No, that one's chronological, no, that's only the reading habits, no, that one's to do with the running of the house. Where's the master-box now? It's not complete for all notebooks you must understand. I've indexed some but not all, there is so much, I've had to divide it chronologically and under headings, here's the Calverley family, that won't do ... now this might be it ...
'Nothing under LaMotte. No, wait a minute. Here. A cross-reference. We need the reading box. It's very theological, the reading box. It appears –' she drew out a dog-eared yellowing card, the ink blurring into its fuzzy surface – 'it appears she read [the book in question] in 1872.'
She replaced the card in its box, and settled back in her chair, looking across at Roland with the same obfuscating comfortable smile. Roland felt that the notebooks might be bristling with unrecorded observations about Christabel LaMotte that had slipped between Beatrice's web of categories.

More than one needs to know

Kitty, in *Kitty and Virgil* by Paul Bailey (Fourth Estate, 1998) is an indexer by profession, and explains to her lover, Virgil, one of the results of her work:

> 'Tonight I am an expert on the life and mysterious ways of Teresa of Avila. At least I think I am, now that I've supplied the index to a book about her. That's the beauty of my little job, Virgil – the copious knowledge I acquire.'
>
> This year alone she had become a specialist on the English in Sicily in the 19th century; on the first governor-general of Bengal, Warren Hastings – whose grateful biographer had taken her to tea at the Ritz; on the chanteuse Edith Piaf, awash in drink and misery; on – she couldn't keep up with all the subjects on which she was currently an authority – oh yes, the Albigenses, whom she'd had to distinguish between in the four hectic days she and Virgil were separated; on Louis Quinze and Madame du Barry; on the Iron Chancellor, Otto von Bismarck; on the Danish composer Carl Nielsen; on Diaghilev, the impresario, and, and – and on other things and other people, already too numerous to remember.
>
> She was an expert, too – though she had no wish to be – on 'The Times and Crimes', to give the book's sub-title, of a man who modestly styled himself the King of London's Underworld. His unedifying life story had been a torment to index, or rather cross-index, because every one of the King's shady acquaintances possessed two names – the name that was chosen for him at birth and a nickname descriptive of his talent or character. There was 'Big' Jimmy Saynor, for instance, who was always referred to as 'Slasher' in the text. ... 'Growler' Gaisford, Morry 'Icepick' Maddox, and 'Flyweight' Walsh, alias the 'Kilkenny Killer'. ... At this particular moment she knew almost everything anyone needed to know about the King of London's Underworld and his circle – but the moment would pass and she would soon lose some of her unwanted knowledge, she hoped.

When she reads her last, long, complex, reminiscent letter from Virgil, who has left her, she describes it as –

> 'A very difficult manuscript. It has masses of cross-references. The author keeps jumping from one subject to another. I am finding it very hard to keep pace with him. He's provided me with quite a challenge.'

Life is just an index

The August 2000 edition of *Good Housekeeping* magazine included a short story by Deborah Moggach, 'How to Divorce Your Son'. The middle-aged son in question, Martin Jowel, is an indexer. As his mother puts it, 'He compiles indexes for technical books – work about which I find it hard to summon up any interest. It's a dogged sort of job ...', and the story is recounted in indexing terms.

Martin's mental account of his marriage runs:

> Marriage: see under Humiliation. See also under Sex. Sex: see under Infrequency of. See also under Performance, inadequacy of.
> Compiling indexes is the only thing that keeps me sane. Out of chaos, it creates order. There is a certain beauty in it – sorting out priorities, making connections.
> Adultery: see under Newman, Keith. See also under Boots, opportunities for liaisons at.

At the end of the story, settled in a new relationship with Preston, Chesterfield's (male) Librarian, he reflects:

> As I said, an index makes sense of things. Mine does, now. Jowell, Martin: schooldays, see under Bullying; Mother, see under Complicated relationship with; Marriage, see under Misery and Misunderstanding; Happiness in middle years, see under Preston, see under Chesterfield Library, epiphany at, see under Gay, see under joy, see under Relief.
> See under Love.

Acknowledgements

Comments and critiques by other writers are taken from the following sources, reprinted here by permission of the authors (or their heirs) and of the Society of Indexers. They are identified here by chapter then entry numbers.

1: 1 Wellisch, Hans H. The oldest printed indexes. *The Indexer* 15 (2) Oct. 1986, 73-82

1: 4 Johnson, Peter N. W. Printed indexes to early British periodicals. *The Indexer* 16 (3) April 1989, 147-55

1: 6 Anderson, M. D. Bias in Indexing. *The Indexer* 9 (1) April 1974, 27-30

1: 16 Vickers, John A. Index for after-thoughts. *The Indexer* 14 (2) Oct. 1984, 124

1: 17 Kyte, C. H. J. *The Times* index. *The Indexer* 5 (3) Spring 1967, 125-29

1: 23 Vickers, John A. Caliban as indexer. *The Indexer* 16 (3) April 1989, 205

1: 25 Knight, G. Norman. *Indexing, the Art Of*. Allen & Unwin, 1979, 177-8

1: 26 Ibid, 178-9

1: 27 Crane, Ian D. Personal communication

1: 29 Knight, G. Norman. A. P. H.'s humorous indexes. *The Indexer* 6 (3), 108-15

1: 40 Wellisch, Hans H. *Indexing from A to Z*, 2nd edn. H. W. Wilson 1995, 284

1: 45 Wellisch, Ibid, 321

11: 4 Wellisch, Hans H. Lewis Carroll as indexer. *The Indexer* 18 (2) Oct. 1992, 110; and Imholz, August A., Jr. *Indexer nascitur, non fit* - Lewis Carroll as indexer again. *The Indexer* 20 (1) April 1996, 11-13

11: 7 Collison, Robert. *Indexes and Indexing*. 4th edn, Ernest Benn, 1972, 176-77

11: 10 Batchelor, Judy. Review, *The Indexer* 17 (1) April 1990, 72

11: 11 Vickers, John A. First and last lines. *The Indexer* 16 (2), Oct. 1988, 103

11: 12 Batchelor, Judy. Para-index and anti-index. *The Indexer* 16 (3) April 1989, 194

11: 13 Batchelor, Ibid.

111: 3 Anderson, Margaret D. Some personalities: Sherlock Holmes. *The Indexer* 7 (1) Spring 1970, 19-22

111: 4 Lee, J. D. Indexers in fiction. *The Indexer* 14 (1) April 1984, 14

111: 5 Batchelor, Judy. Deer-stalkers and data banks. *The Indexer* 14 (2) Oct. 1984, 121-22

111: 9 Batchelor, Judy. Review, *The Indexer* 17 (1) April 1990, 72

Extracts from indexes and novels are quoted here by permission of the following:

1: 11 Reproduced by permission of Penguin Books Ltd

1: 18 Faber & Faber Ltd

1: 28 The Society of Authors on behalf of the Bernard Shaw estate

1: 30 By permission of Oxford University Press

1: 31 Julian Potter

1: 32 Edinburgh University Press

1: 33 Cambridge University Press

1: 37 Curtis Brown on behalf of Bernard Levin Copyright © by Bernard Levin 1970

1: 39 Copyright Frank Muir 1976. Reproduced by permission of the author c/o Rogers, Coleridge & White Ltd., 20 Powis Mews, London W11 1JN

1: 42 John Murray (Publishers) Ltd

1: 43 Carlton Books

1: 44 Reproduced from the index to *The Diary of Samuel Pepys* edited by Robert Latham and William Matthews (Copyright © The Master, Fellows and Scholars of Magdalene College Cambridge, Robert Latham and the Executors of the Estate of William Matthews) by permission of PFD on behalf of the copyright holders

1: 47 Hunter Davies

1: 48 Dale Spender

1: 51 Extracted from *The Clothes Have no Emperor: A Chronicle of the Reagan Years* by Paul Slansky (NY, Simon & Schuster, 1989)

1: 52 Julian Barnes

1: 54 Nancy Mulvany

11: 8 Reproduced with permission of Curtis Brown Group Ltd, London on behalf of the Estate of E C Bentley. © E C Bentley 1981

11: 9 Excerpts from PALE FIRE by Vladimir Nabokov by arrangement with the Estate of Vladimir Nabokov. All rights reserved

11: 10, and 111: 9 *Life: a User's Manual* by Georges Perec ©

hachette, 1978. English translation © David Bellos, 1987. Reproduced by permission of The Harvill Press

11: 12 Carlton Books

11: 13 Little Brown

11: 14 HarperCollins Publishers Ltd

111: 4 Reproduced by permission of Penguin Books Ltd

111: 6 Hilary Walton

111: 7 The Bertrand Russell Peace Foundation Ltd

111: 10 HarperCollins Publishers Ltd

111: 12 A. P. Watt Ltd on behalf of Graham Swift

111: 13 Penelope Lively

111: 14 Extract from LEWIS PERCY by Anita Brookner published by Jonathan Cape. Used by permission of The Random House Group Limited. / *Lewis Percy* by Anita Brookner (Copyright © Anita Brookner 1989) reproduced by permission of A M Heath & Co. Ltd

111: 15 Extract from POSSESSION by A. S. Byatt published by Chatto & Windus. Used by permission of The Random House Group Limited. / Reproduced from *Possession* by A.S. Byatt (Copyright © A.S. Byatt 1990) by permission of PFD on behalf of A.S. Byatt

111: 16 HarperCollins Publishers Ltd

111: 17 Deborah Moggach

All effort has been made to obtain permissions for extracts quoted. Please contact the publisher should any omission have occurred.

Index